Hidden Among The Stacks

AUTHOR			AUTHOR		
TITLE			TITLE		
DATE DUE	BORROWER'S NAME		DATE DUE	BORROWER'S NAME	
	Anisah Dean			*(signature)*	
	Sarah Coe ♡			Emma Marsico	
	Gianna Trematerra			*(signature)* White	
	Brooke Armitage ♡			Nicole Lanzoni	
	Victoria Orlowski			*(signature)*	
	Nick Zangrilli			*(signature)*	
	Frank Wendling				
	Gabrielle Shockley				
	Shannon McGivney				
	Amanda Brody				
	Robert Vassallo				

Library check out cards for members of the spring 2024 Literature Senior Seminar who began the process of creating *Hidden Among The Stacks*.

Hidden Among The Stacks

The Secret Treasures of a University Library

South Jersey Culture & History Center
2025

Hidden Among The Stacks: The Secret Treasures of a University Library

First Edition published in 2025

Copyright © 2025 by the contributors.
Copyright © 2025 Stockton University, photographs and schematics preserved in the Stockton Archives.

Design and layout copyright © 2025 by the South Jersey Culture & History Center at Stockton University.

All rights reserved. No part of this work may be reproduced or transmitted in any form by any means, electronic or mechanical, including photocopying and recording, or by any information storage or retrieval system without permission in writing from the publisher, except in the case of brief quotations embodied in reviews and certain other non-commercial uses permitted by copyright law.

ISBN: 978-1-947889-26-2

Editing and design completed by Brooke Armitage, Katherine Defouw, Gianna Trematerra. Managing editor and designer, Brooke Armitage.

Jacket cover designed by Jena Brignola.

library.stockton.edu/
stockton.edu/sjchc/

Thanks to Shilo Virginia Previti, Grant McMillan, and Samuel Amendolar for inspiration derived from their work *Campus Building* (2023), a recently published celebration of Merrifield Hall on the campus of the University of North Dakota. Seniors in the Stockton Literature program thought, if Shilo, a Literature program alumna, can celebrate the renovation of a campus building, we can, too.

Contents

Foreword 7

Introduction 11

The Stacks 15
    South Jersey Book Essays, Interviews with Librarians,
    Special Collection Essays, Photos, etc.
    Libraries of NJ Project

Left Behind 149
    An Afternoon in the Library Learning Commons
    The Descent into Darkness: A Ghost Story
    Special Collections and Archives: The Work of Many Hands
    A Letter from Bill Bearden
    Costumes at Stockton
    Construction Documents
    Kindred Spirits

Afterword 191

Index 195

Nothing hidden among these stacks. The upper-level Bjork Library emptied and awaiting renovation.

Foreword

1971 was a crucial year in the history of the Stockton Library, although that was hard to fully recognize at the time. Stockton State College opened its doors in 1971. Early on, the library founded its book collection in part with the purchase of an entire bookstore. The feeling at the time was that the library needed something on the shelves. That year also saw the beginning of the first online cataloging, which within a few years would generate cards for Stockton's catalog and become the basic component of the integrated library system. It also saw the start of Medline, an online index of medical journals still in use. Since that auspicious year, the tale of two formats – paper and digital – began to be written at Stockton.

This fascinating story is told by many people in the pages of this book (an amalgamation of both paper and digital!). The Literature Seniors of spring 2024 had their interest in libraries, and the collections held therein, piqued by Professor Tom Kinsella. For years, students in this program have been involved with works published by the South Jersey Culture & History Center. Essays about some of these publications are contained here. In their coursework, these students used a variety of materials in the library's Special Collections and Archives, discovering that not only did these materials contain stories, but they were also stories themselves: How did these things come to be in the library? Why are they significant?

Special Collections and Archives contains an incredible wealth of items, some dating back to the Revolutionary War era. There are signatures of Richard Stockton, signer of the Declaration of Independence, after whom the university is named. The Stockton University and South Jersey focus of these extensive collections includes an emblematic parasol of college president Vera King Farris, historic photographs and postcards, records of the Pinelands Commission, rare publications on the region's history and even a Monopoly game based on Atlantic City. The compelling story of these collections is woven together beautifully in these pages.

The various authors have written brief essays about South Jersey titles and about collections held within the library. They have also reached out to many of the library staff, asking about their thoughts on libraries in general and the Stockton library in particular. The resulting interviews reveal numerous other aspects of the library's history told by people working in and using the library.

Having worked in libraries since 1975 and as library director at Stockton for eleven years, I have seen astonishing changes. The most significant is the major evolution in accessing information. In 1975, finding information was complex and laborious. Researchers had to use numerous volumes of paper indexes to locate references to journal articles and then begin the search for the paper journals themselves. Locating books was equally time consuming and difficult. Now, in 2024, thousands of items related to a topic can be discovered in a heartbeat by using digital resources. In these 50 years, the research paradigm changed from information scarcity to information overabundance. Part of this story is found in these pages.

The provision of digital content has also dramatically changed libraries. Seeing the inexorable movement from paper to digital form is crucial to understanding the evolution of Stockton's library, and all twenty-first-century libraries for that matter. One reason for developing Special Collections and Archives is the belief that having examples of items in their original format – retaining special books and manuscripts on paper, photographs on slides and prints, paper maps, and three-dimensional artifacts – helps preserve history and provides context for future researchers. It is also true that many items in Special Collections are not available or affordable in digital form.

One aspect of this story that arose in almost every interview was an awareness of the library as place: somewhere for students to be, to study, to meet friends, to investigate collections, to receive information and technology services. This may be due, in part, to the extensive planning process that occurred prior to the renovation now underway.

The goal of all the thought and effort that has gone into growing the Bjork Library of Stockton University, its spaces, collections, resources and services, is best described here by Heather Perez, Special Collections Librarian, when she sees "the light go on in students' eyes as they make connections." This book may help you see this light in others and perhaps provide a little insight from your own reflection.

David Pinto

Student immersed in reading, seemingly hidden among the stacks.

Student and Professor Jack Devine at the card catalog.

Introduction

Within these pages you will find relics, reflections, and musings about the Richard E. Bjork Library of Stockton University. In celebration of the library's past and future – the library is currently undergoing a complete renovation – this book brings to light materials that in recent years have become partially obscured by the technologies of the digital age. We highlight some of the people who keep the library functioning in useful and productive ways, and thank those whom we did not manage to interview. Our aim is to preserve important aspects of the library for future generations to muse upon, as the poets intended. Whether along the Windermere peaks or the shores of Lake Fred, these pages are at the disposal of soulful readers and historians, as well as any person curious about things past.

This is the work of many hands. Most of the contributors took part in the Senior Seminar in Literature taught by Tom Kinsella during spring 2024. You will find our work divided into short essays describing South Jersey publications; interviews with the library staff; and introductions to material held in Special Collections.

Our admiration for Stockton's library and its community is clear to see. We hope we have blended research concerned with the state of modern libraries with the culture of Stockton, past and present. We have found much to praise within the stacks of Stockton's library and are delighted to share our findings with you.

The Literature Seniors of 2024 and friends

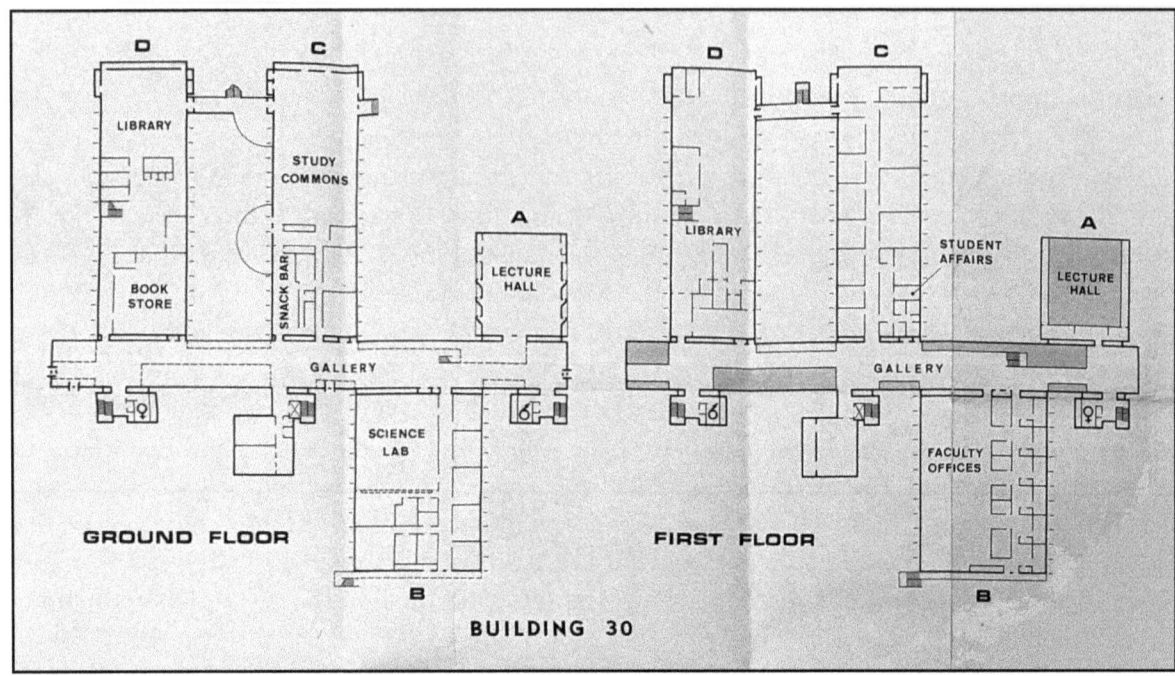

Stockton opened its doors in Atlantic City in September 1971, at the Mayflower Hotel. The first library was housed in a room in the Mayflower. By December of 1971, with the first four wings of the Galloway campus complete, librarians began to move into D-wing. Classes began on the main campus in February 1972. The schematic above, preserved in Special Collections and Archives, shows the general outline of academic buildings at the opening of the campus.

The lower level of the library, 0-level, pre-1995 renovation. Lakeside Lane, seen out the window, has not yet been paved. The west wall of the library is shown at back. Calvin and Susan Kidd, long associated with the Library, identified and explained the location.

Students hard at work at the library card catalog. The photograph dates to the 1980s.

Essays, Interviews, and Introductions

South Jersey titles are highlighted in this section. These titles, published by Stockton's South Jersey Culture & History Center, include republications of important but previously out of print books and titles published for the first time by Stockton's student-staffed local history press. Each is focused, in interesting ways, on the history and culture of South Jersey. Alongside the essays are interviews with the library staff, past and present, and with President Joe Bertolino. The interviews grapple with the questions: What is a library? How are libraries changing? and where does the Bjork Library fit into the Stockton University academic landscape? There are also brief introductions to the wonderfully diverse collections preserved in Special Collections and Archives. Interspersed throughout are images preserved by the library.

Marissa Niceler, Visual Arts major, painting along Carol Slocum's dark path, fall 2024.

A Breath of Fresh Air

An essay on *Seasons*, Dallas Lore Sharp (1915, 2014)

> I have had many a person ask me, "What is the best way to learn about the out of doors?" and I always answer, "Don't try to learn *about* it, but first go out of the house and get into the out of doors. Then open both eyes, use both of your ears, and stand in one place stock still as long as you can; and you will soon know the out of doors itself, which is better than knowing about it."

Reading Dallas Lore Sharp's *Seasons* feels like reliving the moments of my own childhood spent outside. The moments where my friends and I watched tadpoles slowly wriggle into adulthood with the summer sun high and beating down on our backs. The way the sun filters through tree branches or streams from beneath the clouds. Days spent climbing trees, and nights spent on a friend's roof just to look up at the stars and admire their vast expanse across the sky. The fountains frozen over in winter, the snow a star field you could run through or hold in your hands until it melted away. The rainstorms that meant having to wring ourselves dry, and the bird nests built on sills that meant we couldn't open the windows lest we disturb their youngest occupants. *Seasons* feels like unlocking the core memories of the outdoors of childhood and realizing that it does not only belong in the past but also the present.

Seasons is a series of essays that follow the natural flow of life: spring, summer, autumn, winter. In each season, we are presented with snapshots of what makes life so beautiful. The wild, discarded apple tree that has been unpruned for years but protects its visitors and residents – from the cattle that lie in its shade and eat its fruit to the toad who lives within its trunk. The flock of murres who take flight when nature photographers scale the cliff face they call home, startling them away from their nests and eggs, and the brave Mother Murre who stayed behind to protect not only her egg but the eggs of the others of her flock who had fled in fright. The sparrows that crowded the branches in the heart of Boston, heads beneath their wings and facing the wind as, in unison, they meet an oncoming storm. Following animal tracks through a snowy forest and piecing together the story of the creature that left them, not just where the tracks led or who created them.

Dallas Lore Sharp reminds us that the "out of doors" is always near, whether you live in the countryside or a bustling city. ". . . But how quickly the red-green roof of the Library became the top of some great cliff; the droning noise of traffic in the streets, the wash of waves against the rocks; and yonder on the storm-stained sky those wheeling wings, how like the winds of the ocean, and the raucous voices, how they seemed to fill all the city with the sweep and the sound of the sea!" (61).

Nicole Lanzoni

South Jersey nest of the Killdeer. From the Dr. Robert E. Rose collection, Special Collections. These slides contain some of the earliest known color images of the New Jersey Pinelands. The majority of the 62 glass plate slides in this collection are color-positive images, taken of New Jersey flora and fauna in about 1938. Most of the slides are labeled with a description. A few of the images depict people, notably Dr. Rose.

Interview with Jessica Martorano, Access & Engagement Coordinator

Stockton University alumna, Action and Engagement Coordinator, and Supervisor of the Library Student Advisory Board, Jessica Martorano, it is safe to say, has an important role in the library; she is an influencer when it comes to the library renovation. Jess is a Stockton graduate who worked her way from a position in Special Collections to now having an important role in library communications. Jess's new job requires her to get feedback from students, faculty, and staff about the upcoming library renovations and to understand what the community wants to see in its new and improved library.

A recent special project that Jess and student Luke O'Connor undertook involved going to multiple libraries throughout New Jersey and the Delaware Valley to examine what makes them unique and modern and to see how the library at Stockton University compares. It is clear from the presentation they completed in 2023, and from this interview, that the Stockton library is lacking in twenty-first-century services. But both Jess and Luke believe that after the renovation Stockton will rank among the best. Jess hopes to see more modern technology in the library as well as to bring services, such as Special Collections, into the spotlight where they deserve to be.

When asked "What is a library?" Jess responded, "It is a social and intellectual hub . . . a place where information can be shared. It is a place that is interdisciplinary, not just a place for literature students to hang out." Jess shared that one of her hopes for the future library is that there will be more spaces for students to work and meet together, even outside of academic endeavors. She believes that the library can be a fun place and shared some of her fondest memories of creating ridiculous TikToks for the library page (in the best ways possible), an activity that connects the outdated library to the twenty-first century.

When Jess first worked with Luke to create their *Libraries of New Jersey Project*, they never expected it to have such a big impact on the library renovation plans currently underway, but now they are two of the leading voices representing what the students and staff want to see in the future. It is clear that Jess has high expectations for this renovation and believes that the library will be much better than it is now. As a current Literature student who has spent countless hours in our library, I feel reassured knowing that Jess is an important voice, and I know that she will help to make the library more serviceable, inclusive, and welcoming.

Interviewed by Gianna Trematerra

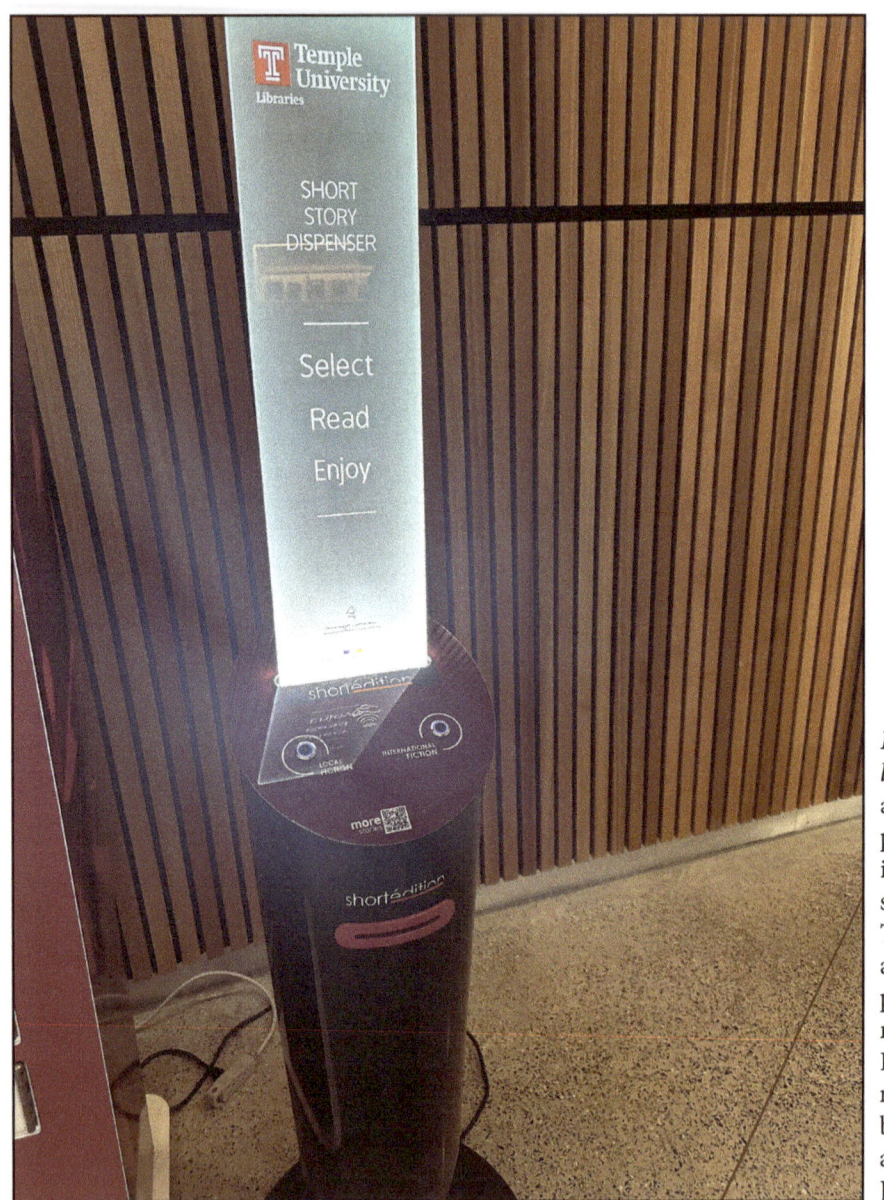

Innovations at neighboring libraries. Short story dispenser at Temple University. With a push of a button, a free story is printed for users: poetry, short stories, and flash fiction. The Temple dispenser features a local fiction button, which prints out stories written by members of the Temple or Philadelphia writing communities. The international fiction button dispenses stories from around the world. Photo by Jessica Martorano.

Waves

I've heard it said that feminism is resurrected every fifty years or so. And while we could sit and argue over whether or not the movement ever really "dies," there's no denying its ebb and flow within the public consciousness, the ever-evolving, radical epistemologies churning in its depths, or those thrilling moments when the squalls of change build up with a ferocity previously unknown, culminating in an awe-inspiring tempest, a mighty *wave* that takes the world by storm. Yes, there's no denying that it comes in waves – and it was the Second Wave that brought me to Stockton University's Special Collections in the Fall of 2023.

The Second Wave of Feminism had always possessed a unique allure to me. Like its predecessors, this wave – which occurred between the early 1960s and late 1970s – sought to reimagine the cultural bounds of womanhood in pursuit of a more equitable society. There is something so radical about the burning bras, the beloved lavender menaces, and the sweet thrill of collective, grassroots action that reminds me that I have a pulse. Revolution, generally, was in the air at this time; previously-colonized nations were working to gain their independence, civil rights and anti-war activism flourished, and sexual liberation reigned supreme. What better time, then, to revolutionize the very fabric of womanhood? I confess that I was in the midst of such a revolution myself when I made my debut as a Documenting South Jersey intern (still am, in a way); one which I've since dubbed "Second Wave Liz-ism." While, unlike my predecessors, I am fortunate enough to have been born in an era that reaps the benefits of previous generations' activism, these benefits were frequently withheld from me until my college years. For nearly two decades, I had lived under the watchful eye of strict Catholic doctrines and the constant threat (and frequent execution of) domestic violence; hyperfemininity was a *must*, any indicator of self-determination was a *must not*, and the performance of docile obedience seemed to be a matter of life and death at times. I didn't even know it was possible for a woman to run for the presidency until the years leading up to the 2016 election, when Hillary Clinton announced her candidacy. But by the time I had reached my final semester at Stockton University, I was fatherless, godless, a child empress charged with the care of my own destiny for the first time in my life. Reader, my revolution was long overdue. You might be wondering why I'm telling you all of this; you are, after all, here to read about the Stockton Library, not my autobiography. However, you will soon come to find, just as I did, that these two histories are irrefutably, inextricably linked.

My task was straightforward enough: peruse Special Collections, search for a story or thread within the collection of my choice, and tease out a short documentary from there. Given my previous involvement with *Stockpot Literary Magazine* and *The Argo*, ever-insatiable hunger for feminist epistemologies, and penchant for all things '70s (I write, as I gaze on the Ziggy Stardust shrine in my bedroom), it only seemed natural to see what *Heracane* and *Spirit of '48* – Stockton State College's Second-Wave feminist student publications – had to offer. Vague curiosity led me to these publications; reverence for what I found within them kept me there. I can still recall the awestruck sensation, the electric buzz running through my fingers as they pressed against the aged newspaper, as I bore my eyes into the opening scrawl of the Winter 1976 issue of *Spirit of '48*, which read:

> In July 1848, the first American Women's Rights convention was held in Seneca Falls, N.Y., "To discuss the social, civil, and religious rights of women." Although the Seneca Falls Convention by no means marks the birthday of the women's movement, it does merit historical distinction [. . .] Perhaps the most significant aspect, however, was the fact that it laid the foundation for future meetings; it allowed women to meet and talk to each other, without fear, about common problems; and it created a certain spirit of solidarity and friendship in struggle, the spirit of '48.

I suppose that assigning divinity to any one person or group of people (and by extension, their work) is an inherently anti-feminist concept. But as I sat there turning through the yellowed sheets of newspaper, poetry journals splayed out before me, I couldn't shake the feeling that I had stumbled upon a holy relic. *Spirit of solidarity and friendship in struggle.* And the spirit was there, practically oozing off each page; it danced in the eyes of each drawn and photographed woman: dirt-covered little girls playing outside, portly old women standing on street corners, rowdy college-aged women who were all limbs and untamed hair and unfiltered, beaming faces. It burned through each stanza of their poetry and bit back at the muzzle-branding hand that would see it quelled in each editorial piece. Its sheer authenticity – a far cry from the pseudo-feminist marketing tactics of modern academia and its dead-eyed poster girl of defanged, performative liberation – made me ache. It is one thing to see tangible evidence of radical feminist activism. It is another thing entirely to see it carried out at your own local college out in the Sticks, in rooms that you've frequented and in communities that you would have otherwise thought to be box office poison for feminist progress – and half a century ago, at that. There was an air of timelessness to these women and their art. It was as if I was looking at photos of my friends and myself, or that the names listed in the table of contents were those of my own colleagues. I felt like a bumbling archivist, sifting slack-jawed through a secret, brilliant history that had been right under my nose this entire time. An entirely new world, hidden in plain sight. And I thought to myself: *why hadn't I known about this before?*

    I'll concede that it was partially my fault. I could give you a thousand excuses, but it all boils down to me simply not looking (or, rather, not knowing that there was something to be looking for). But I think that there are other contributing factors at play, too. Think back to the initial debate over feminism's continued "resurrection" and implied mortality – if feminism *can* die, then what kills it? For starters, the intentional silencing of its history. One of the most effective ways to cripple a movement is to convince its proponents that it is no longer necessary, until it withers and rots like a neglected muscle. We see this in claims that our work is done, and that we live in a "post-feminist" society. But as I delved into the depths of *Spirit of '48* and *Heracane*, it was apparent to me that this is hardly the case. There, printed in these books, were writings and artwork of women who once sat in my very spot, all confronting the same issues that many of us still face: abortion rights, lesbophobia, and sexual assault on campus, to name a few. It is as if we're stuck in a time loop, doomed to forget our predecessors and thereby doomed ourselves to the fates they worked tirelessly to save us from.

    I had the opportunity to meet some of these aforementioned predecessors during my journey through Special Collections by reading through their work; or, in the case of alumna Elizabeth Kelly, by meeting with them in-person. Looking back, I fear that I may have scared Beth a bit. I was practically foaming at the mouth when she kindly accepted my invitation to interview her – and when the day finally came, she had to remind me to breathe every few minutes. Though I often consider myself an articulate, quick-talking person, I found myself speechless in her presence. Similar to how I saw myself reflected on the pages of each publication, I daresay I found myself reflected in Beth, as well. She, too, was once a bespectacled, chubby-cheeked young woman from the pines who underwent her own revolution by pushing the boundaries of what she thought was possible for herself, and in turn contributed significantly to an even bigger revolution. But another thing that had struck me about the interview was when Beth told me that she hadn't thought much about *Heracane* and *Spirit of '48* since her days at Stockton when she contributed to each publication; in fact, she admitted to not having really sat down and thought about her life-long history as an activist within the academy as a whole. This project was not just an act of discovery for me. It was an act of rediscovery for Beth, as well.

But where do Special Collections fit in here? Why should you care? I'll let you in on a little secret – but please, don't treat it as one. Shout it from the rooftops, if you feel so inclined. But know this: the very act of exploring these collections, utilizing archival resources, and rediscovering hidden histories is an act of resistance against the systemic silencing of feminist epistemologies. Yes, Reader, remembrance is a revolutionary act. Because in order to act you must first care about what it is you are acting on. And in order to care, you must know what it is that you are caring for. But to even make it that far, you must remember all that you have learned. So I urge you: get out there, read, remember, care, and act on it. Refuse to be doomed to the cycle of forgetfulness. Embrace the tempest of informed change. Let its waves wash over you.

Liz Myers

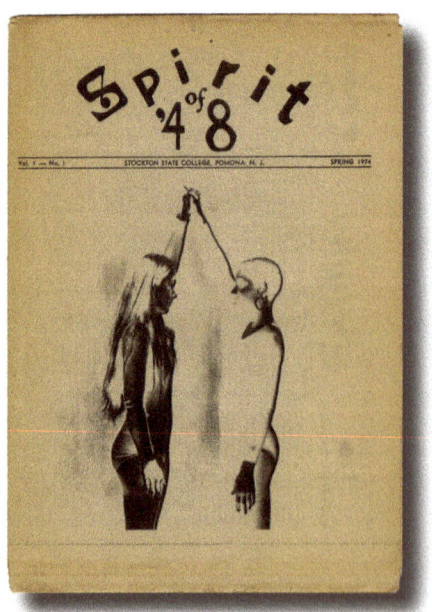 

A Birds Eye View

An essay on *Everyday Adventures*, Samuel Scoville Jr. (1920, 2018)

In today's age of smartphones and social media, the younger generation has taken to watching nature through a screen rather than through the actual great outdoors. This lack of natural experience has caused the younger generation to feel drained of the light feeling that comes from the smell of a cool autumn breeze or from the sound of ocean waves crashing against the shore. They envision grand adventure and explore through video games and Instagram reels because that is what they have grown accustomed and conditioned to.

In Samuel Scoville Jr.'s *Everyday Adventures*, readers become immersed in adventurous journeys with Scoville's friends: the Collector, Banker, and Snakecatcher. Birdwatchers all, these characters climb cliff faces and spend nights in mosquito-ridden beds in pursuit of their quarry – a glimpse of a bird or its nest. Although writing well before the digital age, Scoville clearly suggests through his essays that when you stop experiencing nature through a screen and start exploring the beauty of nature out of doors, it will fill you with more vigor and adventure than a post ever could.

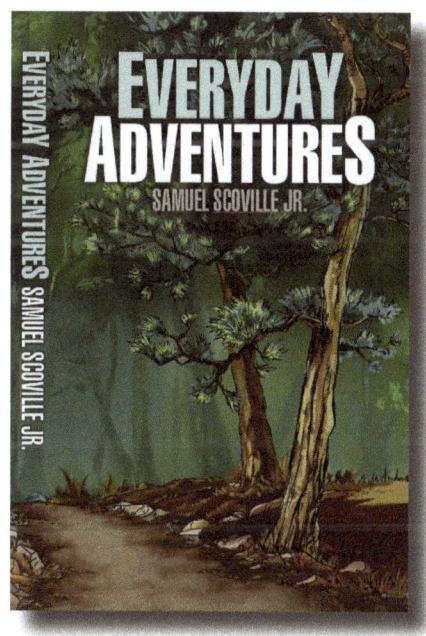

One may thoughtlessly believe that bird watching is not a physically demanding hobby, rather a relaxing venture. However, when birdwatchers are on the prowl for a particular species, they will stop at practically nothing to procure results. In one of his essays, Scoville describes his bizarre ascent up the side of a rocky cliff to see the nest of a Northern Raven with his friend, the Collector. These men stop at nothing to view this nest close up. Through unrelenting rain and snow, they trek the deep forest until they arrive at their destination. Then with little to no hesitation, they climb up a now wet, slippery 100-foot cliff face to view the raven's nest. This wasn't the only time they went to unorthodox lengths to discover bird nests.

In another anecdote, Scoville's friend, the Banker, convinces him to take time off from his law practice to vacation in Maryland so they can spot the Prothonotary Warbler's nest, an extremely rare nest coveted in the birdwatching community. The journey lands Scoville awkward accommodations and a share of a dinner that he describes as "the worst supper that money could buy" (124). Their sleeping quarters held a single mountainous bed and multitudinous mosquitoes. Upon first laying down, Scoville nearly drown inside the bed, and the Banker needed to help create a small crater for them to sleep in throughout the night. The following day they proceed through a muddy swamp in a leaky boat sustained by little more than scraps of the previous night's dinner. The lengths that the people from the birdwatching community will go to procure results are commendable at least and admirable at best.

To Scoville and his friends, birdwatching evokes such passion that the trials and tribulations they encounter are all worthwhile when finally they view the nest of their desire. Throwing caution to the wind in pursuit of a hobby is a trait that everyone can admire. These birdwatchers from a century ago perform stunts that we now experience through video games and movies, and they do so on the mere chance of spotting a bird in its nest. With today's technology, birdwatchers and nature lovers do not need to explore nature to find close-up views of a raven's nest; they can perform a google search and access their bird of choice. For the curious, however, the everyday adventures that you can find in the woods are far more exciting and unique than anything a computer can portray.

Robert Vassallo

To read more about Scoville's works, check out Gianna Trematerra's essay, p. 107.

Interview with Cheyenne Riehl, Student Success Librarian

Frank: What is a library?
Cheyenne: A library is kind of like a home. It's what you need it to be. It's there when you need it, it's there when you don't, and it's available to you at any time. It's somewhere you can go where you have needed information and resources for use, as well as knowledgeable individuals to help you access and find information.

Q: What do you think is the most important thing when it comes to using the library?
A: I am biased [due to being a librarian] because I think librarians are the most important thing. A library is not just a book repository. This is not a place where we just store information; a library is a living document, so it is constantly getting updated, looked at, and reevaluated.

Q: What good experiences have you had with the Stockton library? Have you had any events held there that you hosted or were invited to?
A: Even though I received all my degrees from Rutgers University and have worked at Ivy League universities and Stockton is the first regional/smaller university that I have worked at, I believe my interview was the best memory I have had so far. Coming to Stockton was very welcoming when compared to the big schools that I have worked at. The staff was so nice, the atmosphere was very welcoming. I had this feeling that when you walk into a job you should feel like, "Yes, I belong here and it is home," and that is what I felt when I came to Stockton to work as a Librarian.

Q: How does technology impact your job in the library?
A: Technology in libraries is so important. When you think about the function of the library and what it is here for, it is the first line of providing accessible information and accessibility in general. Throughout time, libraries have been the forefront for technology. The staff of the library were the people that first used some of the technology we have today and have shown people how to use it.

Thinking back, my grandmother was the first person whom I knew who had a computer and she worked at a public library and she knew how to use it before everyone else knew how to use it because that was her job. Right now my personal research is dealing with AI integration into libraries – something I think that people don't think enough about. Technology and libraries go right hand in hand together.

Q: *What do you see in the future of the Stockton Library?*
A: I see a few things being automated because that's just the world we live in. But the library is going to evolve to what we need it to be, so the future of the library depends on what we need for the time. If we need less books and more technology, then so be it. But if we say, "To hell with technology, we need more books," then that's okay too. Maybe that's the way of the future. I think the library is going to be adaptable to whatever the community needs as it thinks about the future. It is what we are going to need tomorrow. What are we going to need in ten years?

Q: *What are some of the positive or negative things that are in the current library?*
A: The spaces and service of the library are positives. We forget that we can walk into the library and do anything we want. You can sit on the floor and we will be cool with it, sleep on the couch and we will be jealous because we want to do that too. I think that varied spaces in the library are positive and important. You don't have to be directly in the public eye, you can go in and study, watch TV, or do anything you want. No one is going to tell you no. The library is the last space where you really get these freedoms.

Q: *If you could create your own layout of the library what would the layout be?*
A: I think a café inside of the library instead of outside of the library [would be nice] because I love to eat when I am studying as well as drink coffee, so I would definitely have something like a Barnes and Noble café area.

I would also suggest more quiet spaces in the library because I think that's one of the hardest things to come by when it comes to being at Stockton University since everything is a lot more collaborative here.

One thing I would definitely do is move the classroom on the second level of the current library to the main level because, for students and myself, it is hard to find. People struggle trying to get to class because they don't know where to go.

Q: How do you envision the reconstructed library contributing to the academic life of Stockton University?
A: It's not what I envision, it is what the community envisions. I have seen most of the plans and it is going to be absolutely amazing. There will be more study rooms, more spaces, and more technology. It is going to be the collaborative space that we need it to be. It is designed for that reason and purpose.

The process of how this library is envisioned all falls on the people and community of Stockton: the staff, the students, the faculty, the librarians themselves, all contribute and have equal weight to how the new library layout is designed. Throughout the design phase, our thought process is to keep all of these people in mind when designing something that is essentially for all of us.

Interviewed by Frank Wendling

Book art, Matt Butenhoff. Photograph by Louise Tillstrom.

The PAC and the Pool

Special Collections and Archives are wonderful and unique. While Special Collections preserve many important documents pertaining to South Jersey history, the Archives preserve documents, images, and digital media pertaining to the origins of Stockton, its development, student life through the years, and academics. With these materials, students can discover how Stockton moved from idea to reality. Two examples of Stockton history that are intriguing to research involve the Performing Arts Center (The PAC) and the old pool.

Both facilities were envisioned for use by the Stockton and local communities. The PAC, a first-class theater venue, provides space for the Theatre program to showcase student productions, as well as traveling musical and theatrical productions. Community members are more than welcome to purchase tickets to the wonderful shows. Interest in the PAC can be gauged by letters preserved in the Archives. When the PAC first opened, local community members who were denied access to a "sold out" show made their feelings known to Stockton administrators:

> Your [Stockton's] cavalier attitude toward those of us who are interested in such activities in South Jersey, has cost your series two rather ardent, but obviously unimportant (in your view), supporters.

Newspaper photographs of the opening night of *The Birds* make it clear that there was a surplus of seating even though workers told community members that the show was "sold out." In reality those empty seats were reserved for invited "local V.I.P.s" who could not attend. The indignation displayed suggests the significance of the PAC to the previously underserved South Jersey community.

Like the PAC, the Stockton pool was cherished by students, staff, and community members alike. Note the use of past tense when referring to the pool, since unlike the PAC, our natatorium no longer exists. If you talk with older students on campus, or staff members, they will share stories about visiting the pool between classes or on days off; some will tell stories about how they came to Stockton as children with their families just to use the pool. Photographs preserved in the Archives show the pool space being used to host a wide range of events. The area was beautiful and well-kept. Sadly, the pool faced structural issues and the cost to correct them was apparently prohibitive. Although the pool is now gone, photographs of students and community members using the pool can still be found in the Stockton Archives. And though we lost the pool, Stockton gained a beautiful art gallery, so at least the space was put to good use.

Details about the Stockton PAC and the pool can be found in the Special Collections and Archives, demonstrating that these archives contain more than just New Jersey history, but also Stockton history.

Gianna Trematerra

The Grass is Greener on the Other Side

An essay on *Garment Workers of South Jersey: Nine Oral Histories* (2016)

In *Garment Workers of South Jersey: Nine Oral Histories*, Dr. Lisa E. Cox and her students present engaging interviews that describe the lives of several women who worked in textile factories in South Jersey. Many of the women who were interviewed came from Italian immigrant families located in Hammonton. Some of these women were single mothers or the sole breadwinners for their families. There are enriching accounts of the lives of the women, both in and out of the factory. Through these accounts, readers gain a sense of the ways in which working class women struggled to survive, but also the glimmer of the joy they found from their work in the factories.

Many of these women had left their families in order to come to America. Franca Fiori Gherardi tells us how sad she was to leave her family behind in Italy to come to America. Since English was not the first language of many immigrants, they were often excluded from job positions other than on farms and in factories. The effects of not being able to speak a language also bled into the kinds of spaces that felt safe to them, including the types of doctors and clinics that they sought out.

Many of these women were not paid hourly, but by the amount of piecework they completed. A few of the women commented on how they would work late hours, in addition to chores and motherly duties, to make ends meet. These women were treated as if they were well-oiled machinery without needs and lives outside of the factory. The total vacation time that they were offered was about one week per year. A week! But while the work was hard, it also was a source of pride. Each specialized in specific areas of tailoring and that specialization made them feel indispensable. Their work was valuable and separated them from the other women.

Many of these women found positive aspects of the job to sustain themselves. Anne Liberto discusses how she worked in a garment factory founded by her grandmother. Liberto reveals how her entire family would be at the factory. She and her brother, when children, used to run around the factory while their grandparents and parents worked. The factory became a communal space. This was important because of the isolation immigrants could feel from American culture and society; communal spaces were places of belonging. For others, they truly enjoyed the work they did. Mary Scarduzio took a lot of pride in working for companies such as Modecraft, Paraflight, and Modern Clothing. She enjoyed her work so much that she wished she could have continued working after retirement, but the shift to garment workers overseas made that impossible.

    Like many women of this era, the women interviewed for *Garment Workers* held complex relationships with the factories in which they labored. Many learned how to survive through their communities, families, and by finding pride in their work. The factories provided not just a job, but a way of life that was both difficult and rewarding. These oral narratives are a testament to the nuances of the lives of the women who worked in the factories, revealing that women's lives during this era were not all doom and gloom.

Victoria Orlowski

Interview with Shekhania Demosthenes, Senior Library Assistant

A library is much more than a building in which books are stored. A library is a second home of sorts, one in which students feel safe to study, learn, and socialize. Many movies depict libraries as stale and desolate, with mean librarians shushing students to be quiet, but this is not the case at Stockton. Stockton's library opens its doors to laughter and creativity and is filled with warm welcomes and kind-hearted staff members. I was able to speak with Shekhania Demosthenes, a Senior Librarian Assistant who works hand-in-hand with Stockton's librarians.

Emma: What is your favorite book or books found in our library (and why)?
Shekhania: My favorite books are children's books. They are my favorite because they can take me away from my responsibilities and stress.

Q: What is your definition of a library?
A: A building or room containing collections of books, periodicals, and sometimes films and recorded music for people to read, borrow, or refer to.

Q: What do you hope remains of the old library? What aspect would you miss?
A: The Plumb and Rose statue and random art pieces like the Dalí card prints.

Q: What do you think is the most important aspect of the library?
A: Our book and periodical collection.

Q: Why did you come to work at Stockton's library?
A: I have a love of books and a disability that no longer allows me to work in a noisy environment.

Q: How does technology impact your job in the library?
A: I do not have to go through a card catalog to ensure a book is in stock. The process has been eased so much.

Q: What does a librarian do? What do you do in the library?
A: An academic librarian's task includes teaching information literacy, aiding students and professors in conducting research, acquiring, organizing and managing library resources, while ensuring that the library meets the needs of all its users. Here at Stockton, they have a niche they concentrate on. My job is to support the librarians by assisting with locating physical books (if they cannot locate them), managing student workers, and assisting patrons.

Interviewed by Emma Marsico

The Plumb and Rose.

Mainland Auxiliary of the Atlantic City Medical Center Records

When I first perused the library's website and scrolled through the list of collections available to view within Special Collections, I imagined that I would sift through photos like those in the Pinelands Folklife Photograph Collection, Robert E. Rose Pinelands Photographs, or the Lake Fred Folk and Craft Festival. I have taken a look through some of the digital collections that are available online and would love to sit in Special Collections for hours to page through the rest of the photographs of local history. However, I scrolled once more through the names of the available collections and found that one caught my eye in particular: Mainland Auxiliary of the Atlantic City Medical Center Records.

I remember AtlantiCare being called ACMC when I was a child and my dad worked at the hospital, so this immediately caught my attention. As someone who works at a local EMS agency, I have also taken frequent trips to Mainland to bring my patients there for further care. Even for those who do not work in healthcare, the hospital is still a staple of this community and shares space with Stockton. Many students and faculty probably even drive through the hospital campus to get to classes every day. I found myself intrigued by what I might learn about Mainland that I didn't know before, and quickly realized that despite having been born at Mainland, having family who worked there, and now frequently bringing my own patients there, I truly know little about its history or the Mainland Auxiliary.

Special Collections Librarian Heather Perez kindly retrieved the two associated boxes of the collection for me, and I spent the next couple hours poring through old newspaper clippings, meeting minutes, pamphlets, brochures, and even a manila envelope of baby bibs and shirts that were housed within those boxes. Additionally, a book she retrieved for me entitled *History of Caring* provided me with the history of the hospital system beginning from its birth in Atlantic City in 1898 when the Atlantic City Hospital opened on 26 South Ohio Ave. It opened in what had once been a private residence and became a ten-bed hospital.

Many years later, Richard E. Bjork, then the president of Stockton and now the namesake of the Stockton library, suggested that the Mainland campus of the hospital be built on acreage that was earmarked for community use at Stockton's Pomona Campus. In November of 1973, ground was broken at Stockton for the hospital on the 40-acre site that was donated by the college. In one of the newspaper articles for the groundbreaking, a photograph can be seen that includes Elizabeth

Alton, a Stockton Trustee and the woman who spearheaded the campaign to establish a four-year college in Southern New Jersey, giving birth to what is now Stockton University. Although I had always been aware that there seemed to be a connection between the hospital and the college, I never realized how intertwined the history of Mainland actually was with Stockton.

Elizabeth Alton and other dignitaries at the groundbreaking for the Atlantic City Medical Center, satellite campus, in 1973, now AtlantiCare Regional Medical Center, Mainland Campus.

Something else I had never known was how involved the Mainland Auxiliary has been with the hospital from the time of its inception. The Auxiliary was formed before the site for the Atlantic City hospital was selected and got to work right away raising money for the hospital. It was immediately very involved with raising money for the Mainland campus as well. Within the numerous newspaper clippings were many detailing the events the Auxiliary was holding. There were annual balls held, fashion shows, community health days, golf tournaments, and even a Spring Fair held at the Atlantic City Racetrack. In more recent years, we can still see the Pike-a-Thon, which is a motorcycle ride through Atlantic County, among other fundraising and community events being held. In its first 35 years, the Auxiliary had donated over $2 million to the hospital to fund education programs, better equipment, and facility upgrades.

The two relatively small boxes that house this collection have given me a greater appreciation for and interest in the kind of material that we have access to thanks to our Special Collections and Archives. Despite the many trips I have taken to Mainland over the last nine years working in EMS, there is so much that I have never known about the hospital's history. I have seen art on the walls at the hospital, yet never realized that in the 1970s the Auxiliary instituted "Art for Sale" – a rotating stock of artwork that is perpetually for sale, with the funds raised contributed to the hospital. Despite the so-far unfulfilled wish from the 1970s that a hospital on Stockton's campus promote a medical school, the robust nursing program at Stockton is a testament to the impact that can be had with a nearby medical system strongly supported and ingrained in the community. Without Special Collections, I would not have known any of this, and I look forward to my next trip to rifle through more local history that I wouldn't have access to otherwise.

Nicole Lanzoni

Natural Changes

An essay on *Seasons in the Pine Barrens*, Miriam S. Moss (2023)

In a world of constant distraction and short attention spans, we rarely take moments to stop and watch nature which surrounds us. The flora and fauna of the natural world are anchored by routine and interdependence. Nature is largely peaceful and adapts only when it must to survive. Society endlessly pushes for more advancements and better ways to achieve them. Have we strayed so far from the roots of human nature that the terms "human" and "nature" now have different meanings? Miriam S. Moss, through roughly three decades of journaling, highlights some of the more neglected aspects of natural and human life.

Moss was raised in suburban Philadelphia and has immersed herself in a busy professional career as a sociologist and gerontologist. Yet, during much of her adult life she resided only a day's drive from a small Pine Barrens cabin, shared by Moss and her partner Syd. Illustrated on the cover of the book, the cabin appears timeless and is described as a small paradise located along the Rancocas Creek. Moss kept her journal from the 1970s to 1990s, organizing entries chronologically through the months and seasons. Moss would refer to her time at the cabin as living in a second world, circling the idea that "this second, simpler world helps me to make a statement – lots of things are unnecessary, less is more, sparseness is fullness" (20).

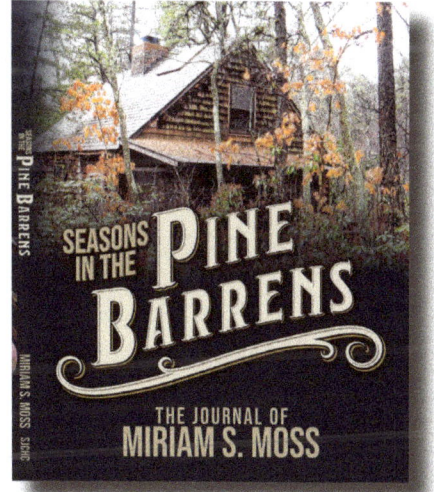

This collection of meditations has no typical plot. Instead, there are Moss's professional and philosophical observations of the seasons' clockwork-like routines. Time is noted in the back-and-forth descriptions of neighbors' passings and the gray hairs that Moss begins to notice on her head, but most often time is referenced through the changing color of leaves and the cycling of seasons. Moss continuously reflects on this passing of time: "People may be born, have worries, joys, and die, but the evening sounds of early May are repeated nightly, yearly. These sounds belong to no one. Others can enjoy them just as I do" (34). Her ability to illustrate the motions that our natural surroundings participate in is so simple, yet shows her acceptance and understanding that plants, animals, and seasons will continue regardless of natural death and decay.

Each journal entry is titled with a single word or short phrase, heading and directing the passage. Accompanied by Moss's photography, these entries provide glimpses of scenes within and around the cabin. A journal entry titled "Change and Consistency" is a meditation on nature's progression and routine:

> I feel a timelessness here at the cabin. Todays are much like yesterdays and tomorrows promise to be similar . . . Why do I get pleasure in these recurrent events in the woods? I am both interested in the novel, as well as the common and expected. Once I see something, I enjoy the familiarity of its recurrence. (127)

What Moss sees throughout her years of journaling is an offering: a lesson that nature will play out in front of your eyes if you are willing to look and listen. It teaches you stability and dependence in the way that flowers know and rely on the bees to pollinate them or moss relies on trees to die for nutrients. Miriam Moss reflects on the current busy world we live in from an opposite "outside" world, using her own experience to provide homage to the simplistic, reliable, and beautiful elements of the New Jersey Pine Barrens.

George White

The photographs on page 40, taken by Miriam S. Moss, can be found in Seasons in the Pine Barrens.

*Interviews with Patricia Thatcher, Dean of the Library,
and Natalie Wadley, Assistant Director, Systems and Technical Services*

*The Venn Diagram Between Accessibility and Relevance,
and How Libraries Define Their Center.*

The relationship between accessibility and relevance is not like that of the chicken and the egg. The need for access does not stem from the latest trend; neither does relevance stem from widespread usage of a commodity or idea. Rather, these ideas are like siblings. At first mention, the twins from *The Shining* come to mind; however, accessibility and relevance are less than identical. After all, accessibility is an equal opportunity for anyone to experience anything and relevance is the connection between as many or as few parts in a whole. Perhaps a better reference image for these ideas are the siblings Bart and Lisa Simpson from *The Simpsons*. Sure, there's some friction in the relationship and one may win over the other (and never let that win go), but ultimately one does not exist without the other.

If accessibility and relevance are like Bart and Lisa – and take your pick which is which – then their intersection, what makes them connected ideas, is the unit in which they are combined. Bart and Lisa are both Simpsons, connected by their name, culture, and upbringing in a nuclear family. The connection between accessibility and relevance is alive and well within public institutions, like libraries, and the societies that support them.

I have had the distinct pleasure of interviewing two local library experts about their relationship with Stockton University's Library ahead of its upcoming renovation. The renovation is considered long overdue by many and has yielded varying reactions and opinions. Here, I will be referencing the two interviews I conducted to examine what the functions of a library are, how these functions affect the patrons, and why libraries are imperative to the societies they support. Additionally, at a micro-level, this essay investigates the relationship between access and relevance for public institutions, such as libraries.

When I first met Dr. Patricia "Pat" Thatcher, she was Associate Provost heading up the Library and Learning Commons. She is now Dean of the Library. Upon first meeting Pat, I admit that I was a little intimidated by the prospect of the interview. I am, in fact, just a girl and I had never interviewed someone before. In addition to that, I was interviewing one of the most important people on Stockton's staff with far more experience than I could imagine having at my age. It was like I was Luke Skywalker, coming face-to-face with Darth Vader for the first time, except instead of having a light saber at the ready, I had a pen and paper (and Pat Thatcher, it turns out, is nothing like Darth Vader).

Upon entering her office, seeing the many tchotchkes around the room, and sitting at the desk that Pat herself had cleared for this interview, I became more comfortable. After all, how could I be intimidated sitting with a self-proclaimed "chaos coordinator," a title Pat identifies with so strongly that it's written on the colorful coffee mug she drank from during the interview? We began the conversation off the record with introductions and small talk before turning on the recorder and diving into the interview.

Pat Thatcher earned her PhD in American Studies and became a historian in 1995. In relation to libraries, she has had much experience in preservation and collection. She has worked in the provost's office in three different institutions and has overseen areas such as student success and tutoring. Pat saw the student perspective through her close work with student populations and within the institutions' libraries.

When asked about her fairly recent hiring at Stockton, she said: "I knew some folks who were here and they said, 'There was a failed search for the library. That's what's open. Could you do that?' And I said, 'Well, yeah, I could do that because I bring student success as a background . . . Yeah, I can do that.' When they said, 'Would you consider it?' I said, 'Let me think about it.' And then I met people here and I said, 'Okay, I'm going to.' It's actually doing much more for students than I had been doing at my previous institution. There's a lot to higher ed administration. So I wanted to get back to more students, with students in mind at least, if not working with them every day."

Pat's previous experiences brought her to a point where student ability and success is now her primary focus. Students must be able to succeed in order to thrive in a permanently changing society. To be successful though, students from all backgrounds and perspectives need access to what privileged students have access to. If there is inequitable access to specific tools and resources, there is a problem: "We like to call students who are in EOF [educational opportunity fund] or in any of those programs or in tutoring 'at risk.' I don't see them that way. I mean, I see them as students who are trying to learn as should all students. So, I see them at an opportunity point where they're ready to learn . . . They're at potential."

Students need the chance to be able to succeed alike in schools and educational institutions. Libraries, as integral parts of such institutions, need equitable accessibility. Pat also believes that libraries function as "repositories of knowledge," where people come to look for knowledge they did not have before. A strong shift within many educational spaces toward group learning gives libraries an enhanced social function as well.

When discussing a library renovation at one of her previous institutions, Pat discusses the combination of these functions: "Students didn't think of the library as only the place to find books or materials, digital or otherwise, to write papers. They wanted to work in that space. They wanted to be in that space. And so it was the creation of a very student-focused space. That included technology . . . But again, it [specialized technology] would be for everybody here, right – the whole push. In libraries since 2000 or 2005 until now, the big word driving us is access. It's not research, it's access."

According to Pat, accessibility is the primary force in educational institutions today. Because there is a shift in understanding libraries as a socio-academic space instead of a primarily academic space, students are spending more time there and must have access to spaces dedicated to various student needs, such as specialized technology (data walls, anatomage tables, virtual reality, etc.), independent and group study spaces, and the tools that fulfill their academic needs while also serving the growing social needs of students. Dr. Thatcher looks to present any future technologies as tools that help students to succeed. Because of her tenacious attitude, optimism for the future, and her desire for equity, I cannot help but to imagine her as a real-life heroine for so many students. A Leia in the face of a revolution, Dr. Patricia Thatcher centralizes what is right by others and fights for it, seeing the positive future that will be.

As I previously asserted, though, accessibility goes hand in hand with relevance. For Natalie Wadley, Assistant Director of Systems and Technical Services, relevance in education is imperative for educational systems to continue to serve students efficiently.

When I first met Natalie, I arrived at her office and noted all the computer towers, screens, tablets, and various other technological tools. She sat behind two monitors at her desk, her face aglow with light from the screens. As far as first impressions go, the image of Velma from *Scooby Doo* immediately comes to mind, with her short hair, round glasses frames, and the immediate feeling that Natalie was on the verge of some brilliant break-in-the-case that would solve all problems.

Natalie told me at the beginning of the interview that she always wanted to be a scientist: someone to take information apart and put it back together in a way that was unexpected. She came to a career in library science after working in libraries to put herself through undergraduate school and, later on, library school. Eventually, she specialized in scientific and religious texts after working for Jesuit and medical libraries for the first two-thirds of her career. She explained to me that her position at these institutions introduced her to technical services, such as cataloging, acquisition, and retention.

Within all this though, Natalie noted different trends within her career: "I guess the most important thing is to stay relevant and needed because we know there's so much more information than people find. In a way, I thought computer algorithms and internet searching would help, but data has shown it's helped silo people. Algorithms are so good at showing and refining things that they know what you like. How do you find other new things? That's been a real problem in terms of, for instance, shopping and politics. How do you find different things? The browsability factor? . . . [It is] the echo chamber effect. It is important to keep libraries as places where you can come and discover new angles to everything. We've tried hard to keep our online catalog doing things like that in terms of being a reach-out on subject headings and showing other things that are nearby."

Natalie explains that current technologies, which use algorithms to collect and track data and trends, often provide duplicative or similar content and information to users, making it difficult to expose people to new information and perspectives. Data can be tracked to determine what users and students have searched for and accessed. Nevertheless, she argues, libraries should not be places where algorithms thrive, but instead places that encourage external research and critical thinking.

Similar to Pat, Natalie identifies libraries as repositories of knowledge, but she sees them as places for her continued learning as well. When asked about the function of library staffers, she says: "We get a lot of education too, just hearing what students are interested in . . . I'm thinking back to last semester when a student came in and she wanted something on some . . . It was some pop music phenomenon. I don't know too much pop music anymore. But we poked around and we found good stuff. So it keeps us exposed to newer things and younger generations' interest . . . So it's not just about the library itself staying relevant. It's also about the staffers maintaining [relevance]."

Natalie remains curious and wants to stay on the same page as the students who seek out her expertise. Her anecdote suggests that she is not only helping the rest of the gang look for clues to see who is under the mask, but also finding clues to solve her own mysteries.

But the data, those clues, centralize what is popular and what is relevant. Natalie uses this data to form opinions and to make decisions within and outside of her career. As one example, she explains that data helps the staff evaluate the longevity of the texts and other items kept inside of the library:

"It's like the older generations of librarians, they kept for the ages. It was a good book, it was a physical book. They planned on keeping it 50 years, 100 years. It's just not possible these days. There's just not the interest in it. We're not a research school that's collecting for the ages, except for our Special Collections and Archives. Back 20, 25 years ago, we were circulating 30 to 40,000 books a year out of this library. In the twenty-teens, we started circulating maybe 10 to 14,000 items a year. Since Covid, we're only circulating 7 to 8,000 items a year. Something's got to give if we want room for other things, more classrooms, more group space."

Natalie outlines that, in recent years, trends within libraries have changed drastically. This is because student needs have changed with evolving technologies. While some of these mystery machines may be unknown to older generations, younger generations become familiarized with new technologies in their grade school experiences. For example, students in local middle and high schools are making tools and toys out of 3D printed materials. In addition, more and more industries are using these new technologies. Today, many architects use 3D printed models to test the integrity of their work ahead of the final build. Since students get this exposure in the middle grades and adults use the technology in day to day work, a lack of the technology at the university level becomes a disservice to young adults. Therefore, access to relevant materials becomes a primary focus for university libraries and the communities they support.

Access to relevant materials is the leading reason libraries such as Stockton's are important. Students come to a university from a variety of backgrounds and for a variety of reasons. Some come from backgrounds where their schools have access to the newest computer systems running the latest programs, but others come from schools with history books over twenty years old. Having a university library with relevant amenities bridges the experience gap between the *haves* and *have nots* in education. Further, the experiences that students can have with such materials give them an added advantage when it becomes time to enter the professional world. Students are no longer being singled out and relegated to the same social space for their entire lives; they are able to move up and out of the space because of experiences that universities, and university libraries, provide.

Students, though, are only able to move into those upper echelons when the services they have access to are relevant and useful. The need for these services is what drives progressive programs, like the library renovation, in the first place. Because society changes minute-by-minute, what is relevant and what is accessible also changes. In order to serve ourselves and move forward, accessibility and relevance must be constantly assessed and maintained.

There's a line from the criminally underrated film *Meet The Robinsons* (2007) that embodies the idea of progress as the basis for changes like these. It goes: "Around here, we don't look backwards for very long. We keep moving forward, opening new doors and doing new things because we are curious . . . and curiosity keeps leading us down new paths."

The quotation has been attributed to Walt Disney, but the film contextualizes it extremely well. A young orphaned boy, Lewis, enters his school's science fair with a machine that will show the user the memory on a specific date. However, a man in a bowler from the future comes to steal the invention, and a boy, Wilbur, follows The Bowler Hat Guy to prevent his actions. Through hilarity, hijinks, and a whole lot of love, the film talks about how access and relevance brings students to the paths they are meant to be on. It also proves that actions in the present affect actions in the future. We must look at what is in front of us now, what is accessible and relevant, to see the choices we have today that will make a better tomorrow.

Interviewed by Gabrielle Shockley

January 7, 1972

MEMORANDUM

TO: Richard E. Bjork
FROM: Steve Nagiewicz
SUBJECT: EXPENSES

On a recent trip to Camden County College for the Governor's Liaison Committee, I incurred traveling expenses and I would like to be reimbursed.

Round trip   100 miles @ 10¢ a mile $10.00
Dinner   3.50

                              TOTAL $13.50

Thank you.

bcc

To: Faculty   April 18, 1972
From: Anthony Marino
Re: Some Thoughts on Faculty Evaluation Prior to Friday's Meeting

    As a result of last Friday's faculty meeting it is my impression that some faculty are working on specific proposals for a more satisfactory evaluation procedure. In my capacity as a member of both the Faculty Committee on Administrative Working Paper IV and the Faculty Committee on Student Evaluation of Teaching I have been "forced" to give these matters much thought over the last few months. Thus perhaps I have some ideas to pass on to those working on various proposals. Here they are.

    The procedures for evaluation proposed by the Faculty Committee on Administrative Working Paper IV are "different" because we appreciated the fact that our goals were different than those of the average school. We took as a given not only that teaching was an important activity of the Stockton professor, but that it was his or her most important professional function. Once one takes this as a "given," traditional procedures for evaluation are no longer very meaningful. To be in a position to evaluate teaching for purposes of retention, promotion, and tenure it seems to follow that student feedback becomes imperative. That data must be collected, or there will be no basis for making any worthwhile decisions concerning teaching ability. Of course other data may supplement student input, such as peer evaluation of teaching garnered through team teaching, class visitation, taping of classes, faculty colloquia, attendance at special lectures, etc. But student input would always remain most critical simply because professors spend most of their time teaching students, not other professors. A professor's classroom performance, unlike his bedroom performance, is no longer an activity inappropriate for outsiders to evaluate.

    If we affirm teaching is our most important activity and thus should be the most critical variable in the evaluation process, and if we affirm that student input is imperative, it again seems to follow that students should also have a say in the actual decision-making process for retention, promotion, and tenure. To someone who asks why, I respond why not? Most of the objections one makes against having students in on the decision-making process also apply to having anyone (faculty and administrators) in on the process. Students may be capricious, but so may faculty. Students may be politically motivated, but so may faculty. And so on. Since so few schools have allowed students to have a meaningful voice in the evaluation process it is mere speculation, not empirically verified fact, to assume that students would act "strangely."

    One of the most frequently encountered objections to students having a role in the decision-making process is that unlike faculty or administrators, they lack commitment to the institution, they are apathetic. This argument brings to mind the assertion of the Southern politician that blacks obviously don't care because they

Early administrative records preserved in the Stockton Archives. These two, with many others, were salvaged from the remains of the President's cabin, burned by arsonist(s) in 1973.

The Sound Heard Around the World
Or At Least Around Stockton's Campus

Since the 1970s, Stockton has had unique creative and artistic voices. The literary magazines on campus – the written works representing Stockton to a wider community – have been unhindered and loud. In the early '70s, the first literary magazine *Crying Voices and Unheard Sounds* was published, the predecessor to *Stockpot*. Other Stockton literary magazines include *Divergently*, "an anthology of student's fiction selected from the creative writing workshops at the Richard Stockton College of NJ," and *Our Stories, Our Selves*, a series of creative nonfiction pieces by students and faculty which drew on the lives of the writers. Celebrating its 50th anniversary in 2024, *Stockpot* is the premier example demonstrating that literary magazines have remained an important and consistent part of Stockton life and culture.

Stockpot is the culmination of mostly student efforts, although faculty and alumni have been regular contributors. *Stockpot* sees alumni return again and again to support the journal. The literary magazines are made up of poetry, prose (ranging from fiction to nonfiction), photography, and art, which consists of digital work, paintings, drawings, etc. Our beloved Lake Fred appears almost to be an honorary contributor as it so often graces our poetry and our photography.

Stockpot provides a window not just into Stockton culture, but also into South Jersey. Boardwalk and Atlantic City life seep into the poetry and photography. In *Stockpot 2024*, one photographer, who is also a managing editor, captures the benches on the boardwalk, the alleyways, and the storefronts of A.C. Through her black and white photos, she preserves a snapshot of Atlantic City that artists can review in future years to see the ways that the city has changed or remained the same. *Stockpot* provides a lens through which we can discover ways that people and places change, whether that change be physical or metaphorical. By highlighting common values and interests, it also shows what has remained the same over the years. Preserving small errors of grammar and typography but also timeless themes of heartbreak, love, grief, longing, healing, and politics of identity, Stockton's literary magazines are important artifacts representing the voices that have made up our community.

Writers grapple with the concept of youth, and innocence, and what it is to lose the slippery eel of childhood. Audiences see what things frighten and excite Stockton students about growing up – young adults emerging into adulthood: from not having enough shampoo to moving out for the first time. Is it not a testament to the beauty of art and human nature that the same feelings can be described in vastly different and distinct ways? Even the title of *Crying Voices and Unheard Sounds* reflects a longing to be heard and pays homage to the feelings that provoke people to reach for their writing utensils instead of their pillows.

From changes in literary style to changes in editorial staffs – from the early, predominantly male editorial staff to today's staff, driven by queer women – Stockton's literary magazines are a reflection of both social change and a testament to the unchanging facets of being a college student and a human.

Victoria Orlowski

 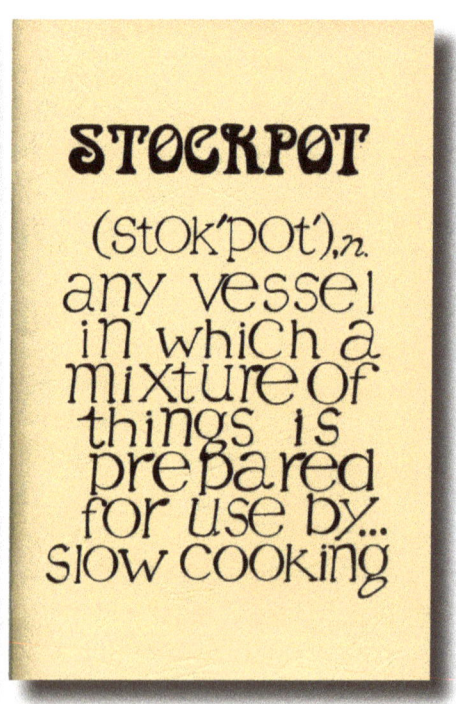

The first issue of *Crying Voices*, spring 1973.   The first issue of *Stockpot*, fall 1975.

Idealism, Inspiration, and Motivation

An essay on *Adventures in Idealism*, Katharine Sabsovich (1922, 2021)

In *Adventures in Idealism*, Katharine Sabsovich details the life of her husband Hirsch Loeb Sabsovich, the founder of Woodbine, New Jersey. While the bulk of the narrative describes Sabsovich's efforts to establish the agricultural colony at Woodbine and also the agricultural school, the opening pages of *Adventures* provide striking views of the life of a Russian Jew.

Readers learn about the hardships and struggles that Sabsovich endured as a child: growing up without a father, being raised by a hard-working single mother, and having many siblings. Eventually, as a young man, Sabsovich began to pursue a career in law, but as he was entering his final year in law school, he realized that he wanted a more meaningful path in life. At that time, antisemitism was a widespread feature of university culture and of the wider Russian community.

Sabsovich decided to pursue the study of agronomy (soil science and farming techniques) and enrolled in the polytechnic institute at Zurich, Switzerland. Influenced by the back to the land ideas of his day, he wanted to prove that Jews could be productive members of society, making useful contributions to fundamental areas of human existence, such as agriculture.

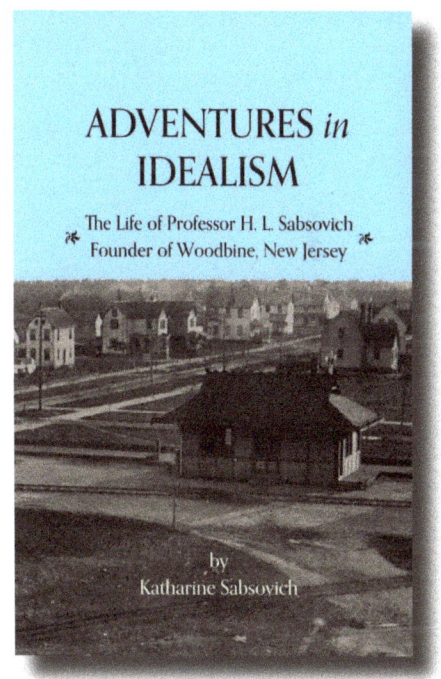

In 1888 after receiving his degree, Sabsovich was hired to oversee a 2000-acre estate in eastern Russia, but before accepting the position, Sabsovich reminded the estate owner that he was Jewish. He was assured that the owner "was above the question of race and creed" and that he would "put character and manhood above all" (39). No one would interfere with his work.

Unfortunately, not all Russians were as enlightened as this employer. The peasants who worked the estate were treated with kindness by Sabsovich who taught them many ways to improve their farming methods. But some could not see beyond old prejudices. On a visit to the estate, Sabsovich's young nephew vandalized an idol of St. Nicholas, affronting one of the peasants. When that same peasant's daughter died a few days later, the mood in the community turned dark. The nephew and Sabsovich's family were accused of cursing the girl. In a moving scene, community elders rose to Sabsovich's defense and calmed what in other cases might have ignited a pogrom.

Sabsovich's time at this estate came to an abrupt end when the estate owner's father, an orthodox priest, discovered that the manager of his son's estate was Jewish. He began to pressure his son and despite the earlier claim to be "above the question of race and creed," the estate owner was not. Sabsovich realized that it was time to move on. Thus, he and family moved to the United States where his skills were recognized and appreciated. In many ways, H. L. Sabsovich is rightfully seen as an early champion of Jewish agriculture and the scientific study of agriculture in America.

As a young man Sabsovich considered the study of law because of the financial stability it could provide. He chose instead to prove that Jewish immigrants could be productive citizens in the honorable profession of farming. Katharine Sabsovich's moving biography of her husband demonstrates that even when the cards are against you, when many wish you ill, you can still accomplish your dreams.

Frank Wendling

Interview with Patt Martinelli,
Retired curator of the Vineland Historical and Antiquarian Society

Patricia Martinelli, Patt, who spent much of the twenty-first century working as curator for the Vineland Historical and Antiquarian Society, began her working years as a Library Assistant in Periodicals at Stockton in 1972, shortly after Stockton State College opened. At the time, she had no expectations of ever going to college, as careers for women at that time were limited. Typically, women could be teachers, nurses, or librarians, as long as they were willing to ignore criticism for not being a stay at home wife and mother. For Patt, none of these futures seemed particularly appealing, but she didn't feel right in college either. She was deeply intimidated by all the academics making use of the library until she met Professor Demetrios Constantelos, whose name you may recognize if you've spent time on the upper level of the library. He encouraged Patt to sit in on his classes and, ultimately, to go to college and get a degree.

According to Patt, the library was the best thing that ever happened to her. Not only did it ultimately lead to her getting her degree, it allowed her to "soak up knowledge like a sponge," something she hopes the library still encourages today. She told me that the most important part of the library is the knowledge that it makes accessible for students and community members who may not be exposed to it otherwise. The library is not merely a location on campus, or a place of background support for students.

By enabling students to learn and encouraging them to think critically, the library serves as the heart of the university, fostering the essence of its academic goals. As the old rhyme goes, you "go to college to get more knowledge," and that is exactly what the library enables. Patt says that libraries today are in a state of turmoil, with an ever-changing technological landscape and rapidly disappearing funding, but libraries still fulfill a key need of any community: helping the community to learn, and more importantly, to grow.

She shared that as the library reimagines itself, she hopes that it keeps its roots. It needs to provide a place for students to study, yes, but more importantly to be exposed to art, literature, and knowledge that they may not have access to otherwise. The library is the center of the community: a place to learn and grow. Patt believes that all students deserve to have a space dedicated to the arts, literature, and culture, and that libraries, especially Stockton's library, should fulfill this need.

As the interview ended, I realized that our discussion had melded past and present. Through Patt, and other so-called "old timers," we can see what the library once was like. We can find what we need to keep, what we should bring back, and perhaps what can be left in memories and interviews like this one, but should never be discarded.

Interviewed by Sarah Coe

Weeding the Reference Collection. Outmoded paper bibliographies on their way to eternity. Where do past and present meet? In the dumpster? In the library? Or only in our memories?

The Lower Level, Don't Call it the Basement

If passion about South Jersey history was a person, it would be Tom Kinsella. Though his enthusiasm may not be shared by all students and staff, Tom's commitment to educating the world around him about the fascinating (and at times mundane) history of southern New Jersey has never wavered. As a cheerleader for *Lines on the Pines*, an event celebrating the New Jersey Pine Barrens (the brainchild of Linda and Jim Stanton), and a supervisor of many local history internships, all focused on South Jersey, Tom remains an important advocate for our community's past.

If passion about South Jersey history was a place, it would be Stockton's Special Collections, another aspect of the local history landscape for which Tom is a strong promoter. In spring of 2023, I experienced my first Kinsella class. In *Introduction to Literary Research*, Tom introduced the class to the many worlds of Stockton's library. Our final assignment was to create a presentation centered on an assemblage of items within Special Collections. This one-of-a-kind space hidden deep within the "lower level" of the library felt like a secret that Tom had let us in on. I remember thinking, how had no other professor bothered to mention this gem of information? Why weren't students being led here religiously, studying at its tables as if worshiping the Gods of South Jersey's past?

You may be wondering, what is so special about these "Special Collections"? The answer cannot be simply put, as it is not only the materials that are preserved, but the people behind and within them that make these collections special. Ranging from Atlantic City African American Oral Histories, to the *Women's Coalition Press Newsletter Collection* (1976–1983), collections within the library hold valuable and interesting information about the people of South Jersey who came before us. According to a brief history of the collections, "Special Collections and Archives, Bjork Library, Stockton University: The Work of Many Hands" (see page 159), this mass of information began humbly as a small file in 1971, eventually growing to the significant collection it is today.

Heather Perez, Special Collections Librarian, and the person who stands with Kinsella in her passion for these materials, works diligently collecting, analyzing, and digitizing the collections for future use. When asked about her hopes for this section in our newly renovated library she said,

For the collection specifically, I would make sure that we had climate-controlled cold storage with no windows. I would also make sure we had plenty of storage room to expand over the next 50 years at least. If money really wasn't an issue, I'd have us build a new building for the library with a whole floor for Special Collections, complete with a large gallery/exhibit space.

Given the importance of documenting history, it would be beneficial to both students and the community if Heather's dream were to materialize. There is no doubt that professors like Kinsella and librarians like Perez continue to stimulate an interest for the culture of South Jersey's past, investing much more into its future.

Danielle Palumbo

> San Jose, Cal., Jan. 9, 1902.
>
> Dear Sir:-
>
> We take great pleasure in sending you a free sample of Weeks' Break-Up-A-Cold Tablets.
>
> It is just such a preparation as nearly every one has an occasion to use during the fall, winter and spring for Coughs, Colds and La Grippe.
>
> It is put up in chocolate coated tablets and is pleasant to the taste.
>
> It is composed of Quinine, Ipecac and Cascara, in fact it is an up-to-date prescription, that has the endorsement of thousands of the best physicians in the country.
>
> Kindly give this free sample of Break-Up-A-Cold Tablets a trial when in need of a remedy of this kind.
>
> You will find it to be an excellent remedy for constipation, headache and neuralgia. Should you want more of it, we can supply you with it at 25 cents per box.
>
> We would be pleased to supply you with anything in our line.
>
> Yours truly,
> FISCHER & PELLERANO,
> 35 South First St.

A cold call letter sent to Willis J. Buzby, proprietor of Buzby's General Store in Chatsworth, New Jersey: "the capital of the Pine Barrens." This hopeful missive, among other documents, illuminates the workings of a small country store at the turn of the twentieth century. It is part of the Buzby's Chatsworth General Store Collection, preserved in Special Collections and Archives.

Family Matters

An essay on *Lantern on the Plow*, George Agnew Chamberlain (1924, 2023)

George Agnew Chamberlain's *The Lantern on the Plow* combines the ideas of duty and destiny. Through a plot that involves interrelated love triangles, Chamberlain examines the ideal of "duty" and finds that people can indeed be "dutiful" and thus can honor the past, present, and future. To modern readers, such rigid adherence to the idea of duty seems antiquated, but these ideas are worth attending to.

Each character in *The Lantern on the Plow* has their own perspective on what it means to be dutiful. With masterful characterization, the first half of the novel focuses on the dynamic between Judge William Alder, Eunice Sherborne, and James "Tryer" Mattis. Prompted by a peculiar legal case involving children and their lack of schooling, Judge Alder pays a visit to Rattling Run Farms, owned by the Sherborne family for many generations. Through his visits, Judge Alder befriends Warner Sherborne, Eunice's husband. The Judge admires Warner's strong sense of familial duty to members past and present, exemplified by his habit of plowing the fields by lantern late into the night. Warner's sudden death leaves Eunice and the children on their own with nothing but the farm to provide stability. Judge Alder takes Warner's duty upon himself to keep the family safe and secure. Meanwhile, James "Tryer" Mattis sets his sights on the property and the family, believing that it is Eunice's duty to marry him for all he has done for the farm.

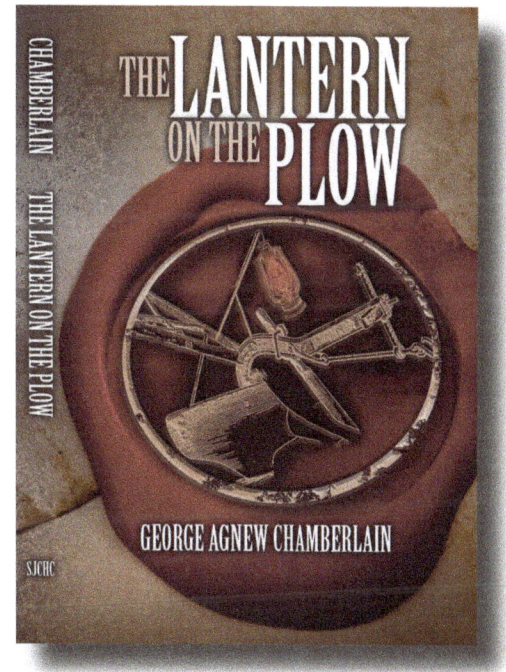

Duty's influence is remarkably explicit in the characterization of these individuals. For Eunice, duty is self-sacrifice in the name of husband and children. For Alder, his duty is unconditional service to others. For Tryer, it is what is owed to him. Central to the story, Warner's sense of duty includes commitment to ancestors past and descendants to come. When comparing these ideals between characters, it is no mystery whom Eunice chose when she remarried and why she did so.

In the second half of the novel, the primary focus shifts from Eunice and her suitors to her children who have their own emergent senses of duty. The duty of Drake, the eldest child of Warner and Eunice, emerges quickly and passionately. His duty is to the family farm. Multiple times, young Drake runs home to Rattling Run Fields in order to look over the lands, even though it was against the will of his parents. Drake's sense of duty is remarkably similar to that of his father: to serve the land that his family had served before.

In the novel, Warner and Drake's dutiful regard for Rattling Run Fields – plowing at night and improving the land – honors past, present, and future. It is a balanced and thoughtful view. Modern society might learn from their example. Too often we honor traditional practices at the expense of the future (think of the use of carbon fuels), employ new practices that curb some negative effects (think green initiatives), or choose a new potential future by rejecting Western traditions passed down from our forefathers. Chamberlain's novel, a snapshot of life in early twentieth-century South Jersey, demonstrates that actions can be taken to serve all people, not just those who came before, who are here now, or who will come after. *The Lantern on The Plow* explores the idea of duty to one's self, to family, future, and past. It is about service to those you feel connected to even if you've never met, and it is about the connection to those you may never meet.

Gabrielle Shockley

Interview with Gus Stamatopolous,
Director, Library & Learning Commons Operations

Nick: So what are you doing in the library? What's your job?
Gus: Presently I'm in charge of Library operations. Basically, I take care of the day-to-day stuff. Communication with text services. Responsibilities within the virtual part. Chief Acquisition Officer which means I get the books, the other electronic content. I touch nearly every part of the operation.

Q: What do you mean by virtual?
A: Virtual to me means not just books only. Library holdings are also the databases whether it is content in journal articles, might be books, might be videos, films, that kind of thing.

Q: What is your definition of a library?
A: The library when I first came to college, when I was a student, was a whole different world. It was all paper. As technology has come aboard, there are more expectations for collaboration amongst students and faculty. I think the library to me is a place where you come to collaborate. We provide a space for you, provide the expertise to help you, navigate those sort of channels. That's the way I see it.

Q: Is having collaboration one of the most important aspects of the library?
A: Yes. My rule here, and the other staff agree, is that we each own part of the operation and help others to navigate that part successfully. We have over 80,000 e-journals. Knowing how to handle those journals depends on what subject you are researching. All the staff, including myself, have responsibilities for part of our holdings: mine is Holocaust studies and Jewish studies and Africana studies as well. We try to specialize our specific areas and provide library users with advice on how to research effectively within that area. You can research a topic forever, but sometimes you need to find just one golden nugget. The research has already been done. Every article has a bibliography; you can look through those articles and get ideas where to go next. Research – we make it a lot harder than it has to be.

Q: How much has technology changed the impact of your job and where do you see it going from here?
A: When I started working in a library as a student, my task was to identify cards from card catalogs (all in paper) and there were two catalogs – one was in call number order and the other was in title order – that was long ago. It has all changed now. The searching part is at your fingertips now. We offer a flash find which is a Google sort of search engine of all the things the Library offers. I didn't have that growing up. Technology is becoming a big part of everything. One of the things we hope to build during the renovation is a data classroom, which will have huge wall-size monitors that provide a virtual experience. That will help students visualize data.

The idea of housing books is going away, although I find books very important. The physical artifact is important, but I don't think you need a library with hundreds of thousands of texts on site . . . As director of Library Operations, it has become natural to be comfortable with technology. When I started, I had to pick up skills on my own. The back end is very technical. We have a system coordinator who does the back end stuff. Technology plays a big part, but I don't want to take out the human component of the library. The librarian here is very important to the whole experience. I can give you technology but what are you going to do with it?

Q: Why did you come to Stockton and how long have you been here?
A: I've been here since 2010. Accepting this job was actually a promotion for me. I was head of access services at Columbia University. I wanted to build my career and saw Stockton as a great opportunity to do so. I came here with added responsibilities. I was intrigued by the database management part. I may be an administrator now, but at one time in my career I was thinking about becoming an electronic resources person, but administrating kept me busy so I stayed there. I really like dealing with electronic databases.

Q: What do you hope remains of the old library? What aspect would you miss?
A: I don't want all books to go away completely. There is going to be a smaller, more concentrated section because we have over 300,000 ebooks available to you on top of our physical holdings. There are certain things we did in the past that I don't miss. I don't miss dealing with all that paper, cards, and paper files. I didn't like doing that. I actually embrace the evolving change that is part of life. I'm not going to really miss anything to tell you the truth.

Q: Do you have a favorite book in the library?
A: Well this library is an academic library. There is not very much recreational reading here. On my own, I read a lot of sci-fi basically. One of my favorite books is *Dune*. The first book was phenomenal. I read it in one sitting. I couldn't put it down.

Q: Do you have a best memory about the library?
A: I actually like our little get togethers we have here with the staff. Holiday parties and celebrations. It's a good group of people that work here. I like working with them. I like being in this social environment.

Q: How big is the team here?
A: It's really not that big. About 23 people.

Q: What do you see as the future of the library?
A: Hopefully, I see it. I'm at the age where I might be here only three more years and retire. Once the renovations are complete I want to see us get closer to some of the academic departments, so students like you can actually work more closely with the librarians. Develop our collections here to offer to students and to let them do research. The collaboration part I think is great. I want a constant review of the services we offer so we don't get left behind when it comes to technology. That would hurt students more than anyone else. One thing that students have been asking for here are podcasting rooms. There is one on the lower level, but it is not controlled by the library. I know we are trying to put another one in the new renovation project so more students will be able to podcast. Podcasting, data visualization rooms, those kind of things really excite me because I think they are going to help Stockton grow as a whole. Every other place I've ever been to, the library is the center focus of the institution and I would like to see that happening more here.

Q: Since the renovation won't finish right away, how do you think the years without access to the library will look?
A: We are going to have space in the C/D Atrium. That's where the main operation is going to be. If you're a freshman or sophomore coming in here, in two years you're going to have a brand new facility. If you're a junior or senior, it's going to be very difficult, but you have to keep in mind,

while you might not have the physical space, you will have the virtual space available to you. The library will be available virtually. We have an interlibrary loan service that can get articles and books that you need which we might not have. The physical structure won't be here, but the idea and services continue. We're still going to have 20,000 books on campus in C-wing next to the C/D Atrium. One of the classrooms will hold the books. Hopefully we won't miss too many beats, and of course renovation projects happen.

Interviewed by Nick Zangrilli

Students Hannah Cullick and Maddy Connelly (front) working with the Alliance Heritage Center Collection in the Special Collections reading room, spring 2023.

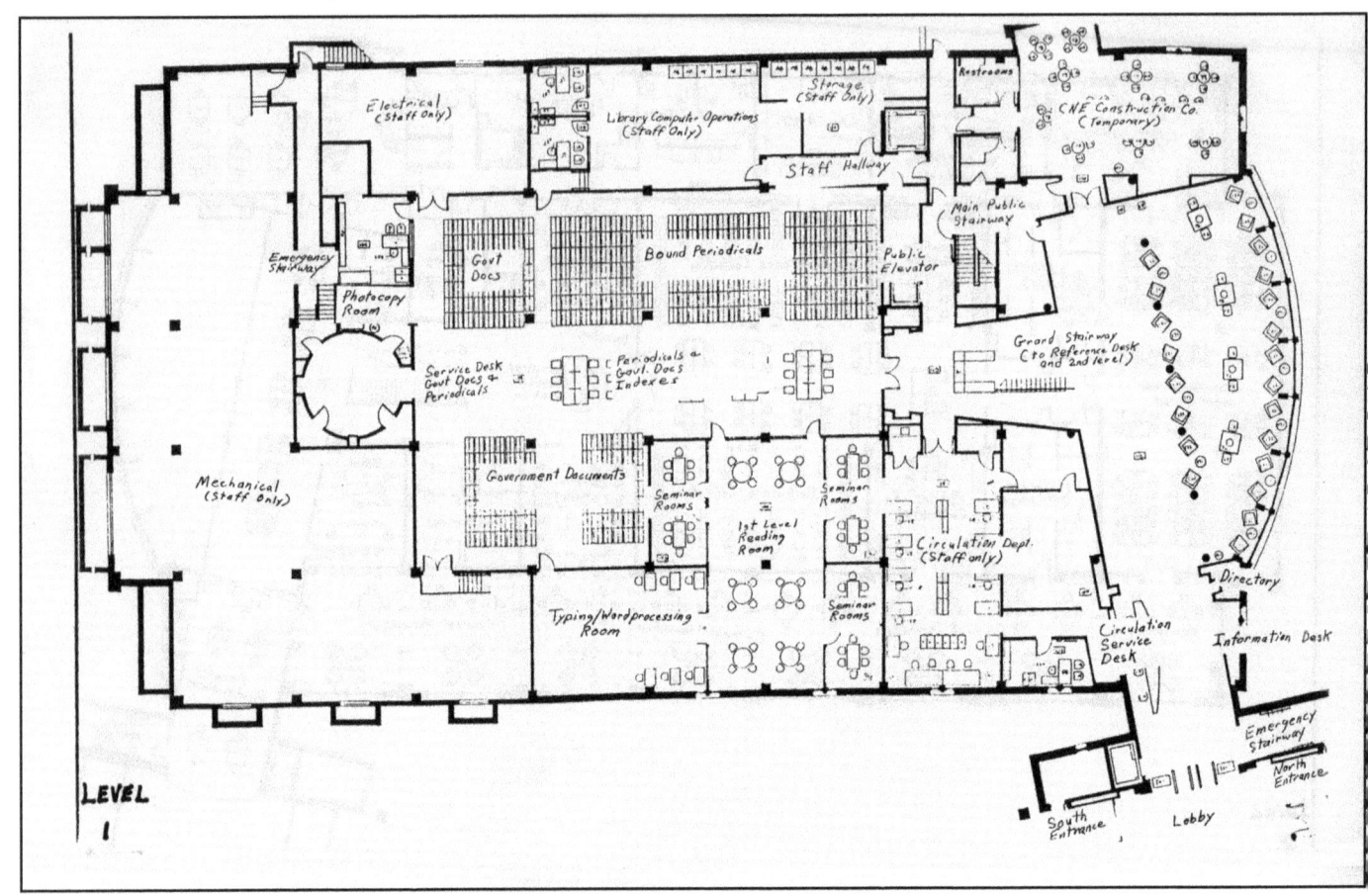

The schematic above and the three that follow, preserved in Special Collections and Archives, apparently show early "dream" plans for the library, c. 1992. The plans were ambitious, with E-wing pushed out on both the east and west sides. The eventual remodeling, completed in 1995 was considerably less ambitious.

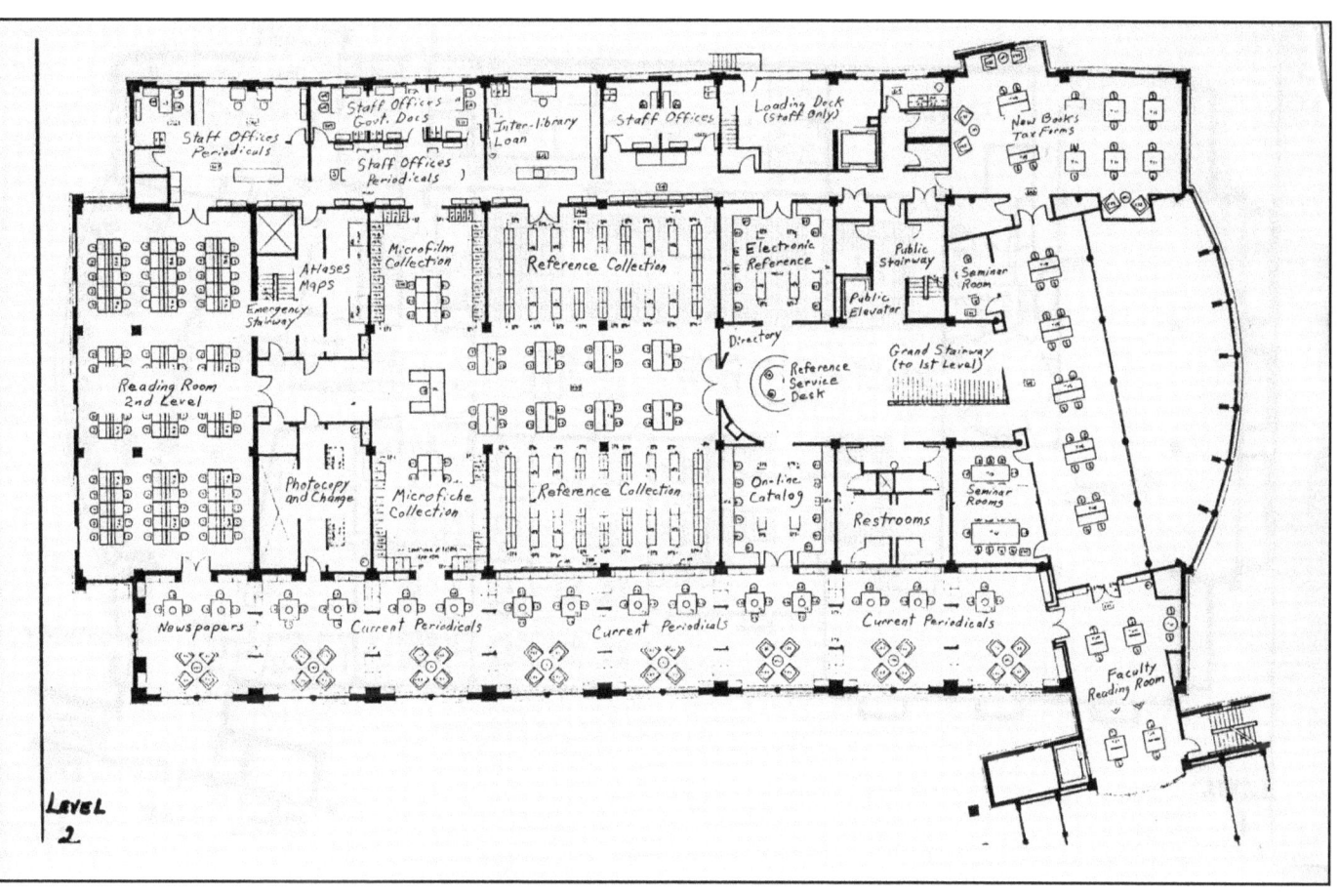

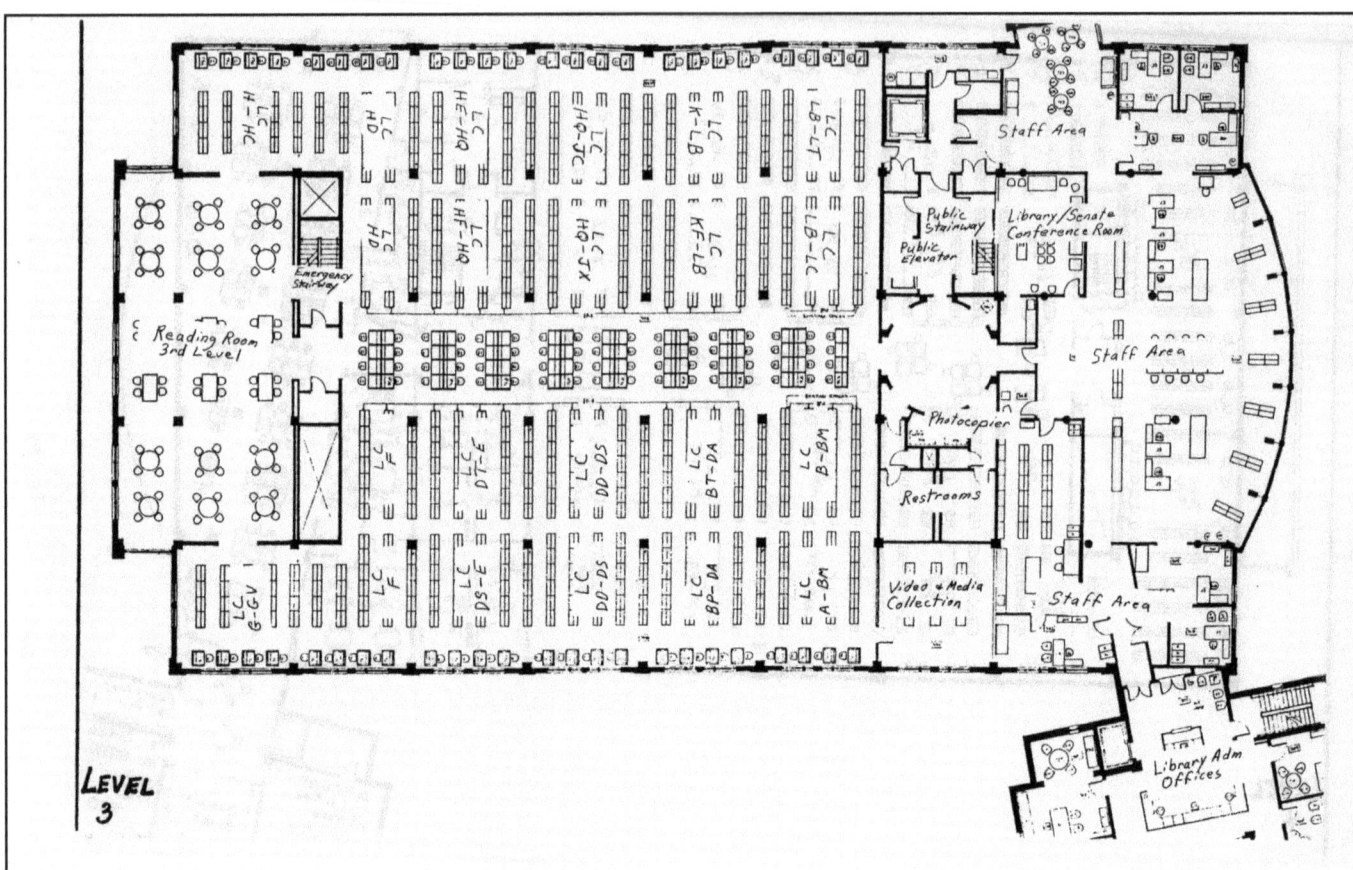

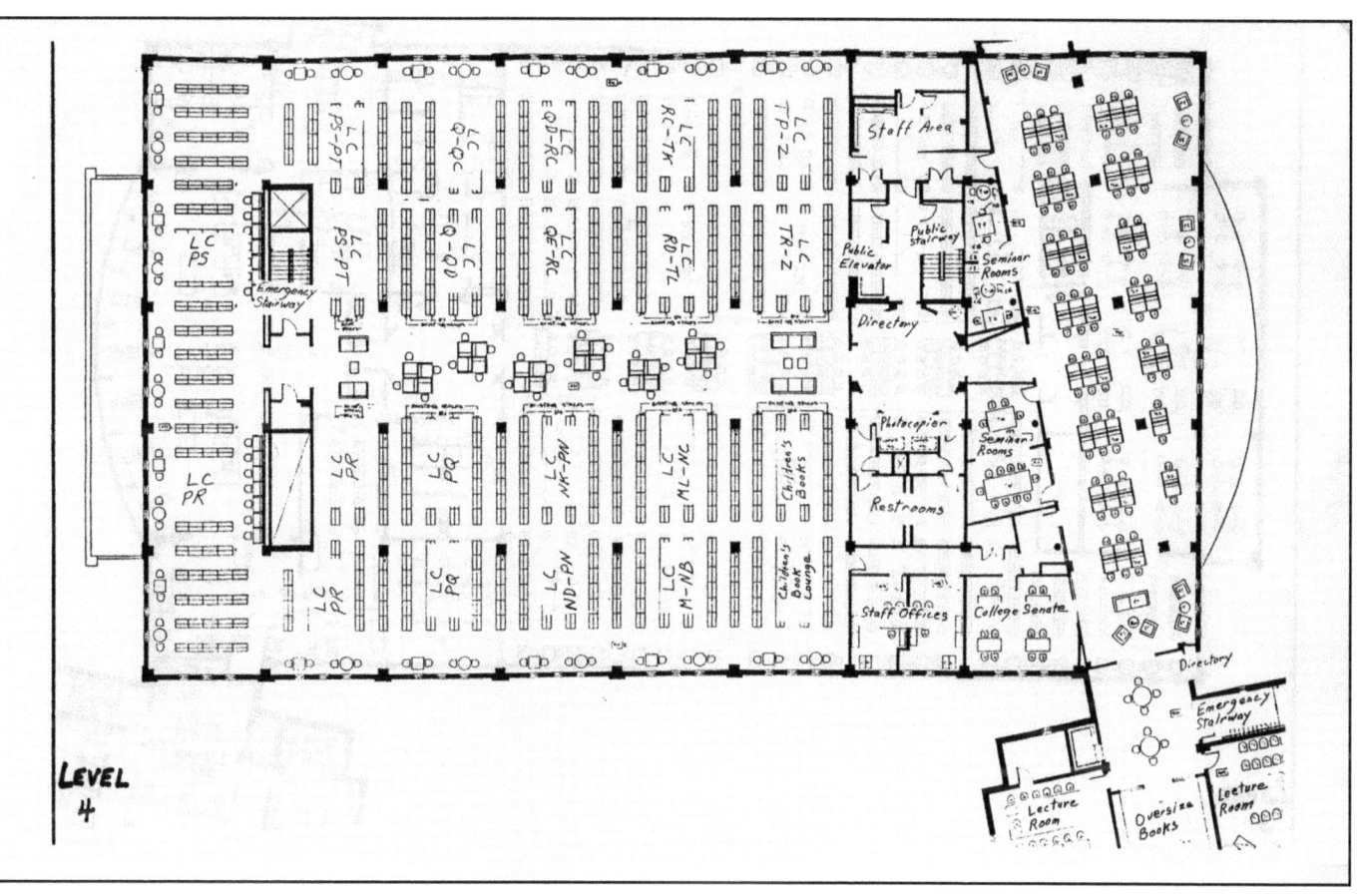

Wordsworth, the newsletter of the library: 1992 and 1995 issues announcing the start and completion of the first library renovation and expansion.

Travel Companion

An essay on *Adventure with Piney Joe: Exploring the New Jersey Pine Barrens Volumes I & II*, Story by William J. Lewis, Illustrations by Shane Tomalinas (2022)

Nature and all its inhabitants hold great beauty. The rustling of leaves, trees swaying in the breeze, plants sprouting, and animals scurrying about. All the wonders of nature are a sight to witness, but you need to immerse yourself in it to truly see. Self-guided adventures certainly allow you to explore nature, but a companion guide offers a fun and more efficient way to explore the natural world.

William J. Lewis provides a well-rounded travel companion in *Adventure with Piney Joe*. Passion, experience, and patience are the foundations of any great traveling companion and Piney Joe, a gnome filled with enthusiasm and knowledge about the New Jersey Pine Barrens, is just such a companion. Our gnome narrator makes trekking through the Pine Barrens an enjoyable experience, highlighting what is truly important to the Pines rather than just listing off scientific facts. Find a partner with the same flair as Piney Joe and you will see nature in a way you never thought possible.

To the unfamiliar, the sights of the Pine Barrens may all look similar – "Look, more trees!" – but William J. Lewis, through his narrating gnome, describes and illustrates dozens of intriguing Pine Barrens plants, providing their common names, making identification and memorization more relatable. Sweet Gum is a lot easier to remember than *Liquidambar styraciflua*. Shane Tomalinas' images in this well illustrated text give the reader a visual cue helping hikers to identify Pine Barrens' plants, making learning about nature less daunting and, more importantly, more enjoyable.

Pineys, the people who reside in the Pine Barrens, play just as big a role in caring for the environment as the flora and fauna. People have lived in the Pine Barrens for centuries, creating ways to maintain a sustainable life. Lewis emphasizes the culture showcased by the Pineys through Piney Joe's enthusiastic attitude toward the land. Exquisite plants and trees that make up the ecological tapestry work hand in hand with those who reside in the Pines. The dried floral industry, for instance, was an early way for the Pineys to make a living. Pineys collected salable floral materials without causing significant ecological harm.

Reading about Lemongrass, Turkey Beard, and Penny Crest is enjoyable and provides valuable information, but seeing them on your own, with an excellent guide, provides a richer experience. William J. Lewis delivers information about the Pine Barrens in ways that are both delightful and accessible, but perhaps his most important lesson is teaching readers to see the Pine Barrens for themselves.

Nicholas Zangrilli

Interview with Charla Comer, Technical Library Assistant

Nicole: So [Professor Kinsella] did send me the previous interview you had done with some Stockton students. I know that you began working here in 1980.
Charla: 1980, yeah.

Q: Do you have any best memories or stories of anything that's happened here or anything that stands out to you? I know it's a lot of years to draw from.
A: Well, if you summed it up, projects. When I came here, the library was smaller. And when they got the addition – there has always been change – there's always been big projects that brought the library staff together as a team. And to me that's the best part of it. We're the whole staff, during these projects we're not as divided – you work in public service, someone else works in technical service. No, we're the whole team. And it's always been the people that you work with. The reason that people stay here is the relationships you make with the people.

Q: Does it usually feel like you guys are more in your own little bubbles in the library where you all have your own things to do and you don't interact as much until there's something new going on, or projects to be done together?
A: There's always interaction between the public and technical service. But when there's a project, like when the library had to barcode all the books for the computer system, then everybody had to take part in it. So, it's something we all did. It's not so divided – like, oh, the public service librarians are working on this, and technical services are working on that. We each have our own, but then we have something that we all do together.

Q: So, when you guys have projects, it lets you interact more as staff, you get to do things more together as a team. That's always really nice.
A: When I came here the feeling was more segmented. Now it's more like we're one unit.

Q: [In your interview for Stockton's 50th you talked about your favorite type of books.] I wonder if it's changed in the last couple years, if your favorite type of books have changed from being cozy murder mysteries? Still the same thing?

A: As you can see, I'm addicted to Court TV.

Q: *Are you?*
A: Yes, I am. It's murder every day, all day.

Q: *When I was a kid, at home we used to always watch* Law and Order, Law and Order SVU, CSI, NCIS.
A: Well, see, that's another thing. I always watch – Tuesdays and Wednesdays are my Channel 12 nights. Tuesdays they have *Finding Your Roots* and of course all the documentaries – *Front Line*, *American Experience*. Wednesdays they have *NOVA Nature*. And you get all the great things about nature, and *Front Line* just re-did an investigation into the Boeing 737 Max plane.

Q: *Yeah, that stuff is crazy. It's really interesting, though. On the one hand, you're like, "Why am I watching this stuff?" But it's just so fascinating.*
A: No, there's nothing I would rather watch. I've always, even as a kid, preferred documentaries to movies. I'm not a movie person.

Q: *I know you like murder mysteries, but do you have a favorite book or books that are found in the library, anything in particular?*
A: No, not really.

Q: *We wanted to know about what your definition of a library is. I know the dictionary could provide a definition, though after having worked in a library for so long, how would you define it?*
A: What makes a library is that it's a place that people come to for all kinds of reasons – for information, for research, for social. There's all kinds of libraries, and in the college library you have a combination of all those things. You have research, you have study, you have social events. In a public library, you have more of the community outreach and programs and things that gear toward families. We always have had to encourage the public to come and use this library, and they do, but our main focus has always been the students. And it should be. It should be the students, faculty, and then the rest of the community.

Q: Do you think that with some of the new renovations that they're doing Stockton is trying to branch out even more and keep going into the public?
A: I have no idea. Because the plan changes.

Q: All the time?
A: Every day. But what it sounds like is they want to restructure the building and put in more services that are already here, but in other locations.

Q: Consolidate everybody together so everybody can really work together. What do you hope remains of the library as it is?
A: What I hope remains is the way the staff works. And because things have always changed here – I mean, from the time I've been here, we went from no computer systems to a lot of computer systems. Things are changing. We're going from fewer print materials to more ebooks and online – everything is mostly online – so that's going to change things. Who knows what the future is going to be as far as what technology is because that changes so rapidly now. But we know we'll change. Libraries always change. Immediately, when the library got the addition [in 1995] the space was taken for other things. That's how it's always really worked. But this is a big change. Like I said, the plan keeps changing so really who knows?

Q: Is there anything you would miss if it were to go, like something in the library that you would miss if they didn't keep it when they do the renovations?
A: I think we're really going to, at the end of the day, miss how many books we currently have. Because so much of that is going to be gone.

Q: Yeah, Professor Kinsella was showing us pictures he had taken of the books when they get turned down and then they get removed. He had some of the dumpster pictures of the books. Most of them are online, but it's weird seeing all those books in a dumpster to be taken somewhere else.
A: We're using a company and they are recycling them. And they're all placing some in other libraries that are interested, so we get a certain little bit of money from discards that we can use to buy new material.

Q: That's a good thing at least. They get a new life, a little bit.
A: But see, that is the thing with libraries. Weeding has always been done. Always. It's something that libraries have to do because even if no renovation were happening, we're not going to get more space. And you cannot possibly keep everything because you're not going to get more space. And things, especially in say science, medicine, anything, history is rewritten so many times. It keeps changing. So, texts become old, out of date.

Q: So, you have to replace some of the old with the new so it keeps updated.
A: Yeah, you don't replace all of the old, but a lot of it will be replaced. We just don't have the room. Nobody, I don't care, the largest library you can think of, will keep everything. Nobody, I don't care where it is, will keep adding building space. Nobody.

Q: Do you prefer actual physical books or have you started to e-read?
A: A combination, really. Depends on what it is. But those little murder mysteries I read on my Kindle.

Q: The Kindle is really convenient for traveling and I really love it for the beach. I don't have to worry about if it gets ruined or if the weather changes or if it gets sand in it. And then I can just bring it along with me. I have a lot of books in my house, but the Kindle is been nice, too.
A: And I listen to Audible, too, because I think they're Kindle books but they were so good. One was about pirates, spies, it was just funny. These were about the history of – one was pirates, and I'm listening to spies now. It's like true history, but they have different people playing their voices and it's really funny, but it's not made up.

Q: That sounds really interesting. I don't listen to a ton of audiobooks. I've only started recently, but it's nice because then you can be driving or cleaning around the house and still listening. What do you think is the most important aspect of the library?
A: I think the most important aspect of the library is the contact staff has with the public, with the students and faculty.

Q: I think that, based on a lot of what you've already said and what you said in your previous interview, the people are really the most important part to you, like the people that you have working relationships

or friendships with here. I think that's the most important part of pretty much any community, the people that you meet and the interactions you get to have with them.
A: Since I've been here, I've had the opportunity to work in other areas. I don't feel like I've been over-supervised. You can pretty much be self-starting as far as that goes, which is great.

Q: I know you're in technical services. Have you worked in other aspects of the library?
A: I've covered the circulation desk back-up, I've worked in interlibrary loan, I was cataloging when I first came here, I've done projects for government documents.

Q: Is there a part that you like working in the most? Or is it just anywhere in the library that you get to be?
A: Not really. I've been in acquisitions for some time now, but the staff is a lot smaller than when I came. When people left, they didn't fill the positions, or they moved them to other areas.

Q: Why did you come to work at Stockton's library?
A: Why did I come here? Oh, because one day I was at this sub shop called Mario's, and I saw a little advertisement for a two-year vocational course to be a library assistant. Now, I always wanted to work in a library, but I didn't want to be a librarian.

Q: I feel like you might have mentioned that in the other interview. It had something to do with the librarian at your high school.
A: Yeah, we were enemies. Anyway, I took that course. And I did my internship at the Vineland Public Library, but at the time you had to live in Vineland to work there. I couldn't live in Vineland on $2 an hour, because back then that was the minimum wage. So, I got the job I could get, which everybody could get back then – working for the Development Center, which wasn't for me. At that time, all the other attendants were taking civil service exams for promotions, and that's where I saw the civil service exam for library assistant, so I took that, then I was offered a job here. So, I came for the interview – it was for cataloging – and the library was smaller then. But I was really like, "Wow, I would really like to work here," but the person from human resources said to me, "Well, I don't think you'll get the job." I was very surprised.

Q: *Didn't get any reason or anything?*
A: No, he said I wouldn't get the job. I was surprised when the cataloger called me and offered me the job, you know?

Q: *Were there any other colleges or universities you had looked at, or was this the only one?*
A: This was the only one.

Q: *What did you do at the developmental center?*
A: I was an attendant. It's not really medical, you just basically work with what they call clients now. You make sure they're dressed, they go to where they have to go, basically watching them and making sure nobody's doing anything dangerous. It's just a very difficult job working with mentally and physically handicapped people who can be pretty violent.

Q: *I understand. I work in healthcare outside of this [being a student] so I understand how that can be.*
A: And so you know what it can be like. Back then, I worked in Pond Cottage. We had over 160 people living in the building. And you had three floors. Some of them during the day would have to be in the rec, and the rec's divided into two, but in the evening you would have everybody moved into one. And you had people with seizures, you had people who were violent, and back then they did finally put restrictions on it, but you would have to put them in restraints. And it's not easy.

Q: *It's not at all. It's really hard to do that, especially when they don't know what's going on. They end up being way stronger than you expect them to be and it's really hard.*
A: Oh no, yeah, we had one who was really strong. She could lift a table, and she would go off. I'll never forget her. She allegedly murdered her grandfather. And the psych ER would just want to talk about it, and she would come back after and be very angry, and she would go off. But then there's a funny story there. The third floor was where the bedrooms were. At night, we would be in the little room folding clothes, and we heard this crying. We would go in and look, and everything would be peaceful and quiet. And then we would go back and we would hear this crying, and then finally we went back and the other ladies had put Betty Lou in restraints

with socks. And they properly tied her. Because she had been jumping up and running down and smacking all the people – running down the row and turning around and smacking all the people. They had enough of it, and they put her in restraints.

Q: How did you know that you wanted to work in a library if the librarian made that very difficult on you in high school?
A: Actually, I spent time in the library. My mom [and I] would always go to the Cumberland County Library or the Bridgeton Library, so I spent a lot of time in the library. For some reason the librarian decided that I wasn't "living up to my potential." So I had to sit in the library, and nobody could talk to me. I was supposed to be studying or whatever, living up to my potential.

Q: What does that even mean? That's such a vague thing to say.
A: I know. "You're not living up to your potential. Here, go over there." Yeah, that's how we became enemies.

Q: So how does technology impact your job in the library?
A: Our library systems are continually changing. Since I've been here, we've been on four library systems. Different kinds of systems have come in. There's all kinds of systems throughout the library. From the time we got our first system till now, it's different, gotten better. But you can expect change.

Q: Kinsella likes to say that you're a librarian in his mind, he calls you a librarian. Clearly you didn't want to be a librarian. So what is your job – library technical assistant?
A: Well, it's changed. When I came here, librarians, primarily the reference librarians, supervised areas. We weren't even allowed to answer questions. The only question we were allowed to answer was, "Where is the bathroom?" So now a lot more is expected of the staff to be able to help the students and answer questions throughout their research and help them with that. Before we weren't allowed, and now the librarians are working on other things and that's why you have to schedule an appointment with them. Other than that, it's expected that staff, and the help desk, and the information desk can help students with their basic needs.

Q: *How would you describe what you do in the library?*
A: Primarily I'm acquisitions, which is now mostly downloading the records of what we purchased, activating the e-books, and other projects. I'll back up circulation if they need me.

Q: *Is there an aspect of what you do that you enjoy the most?*
A: No, not any one thing.

Q: *What do you see as the future of Stockton's library?*
A: I see the library basically changing to – I don't know what it's going to be really. Because they haven't really defined what a learning commons is. The future is a learning commons, but exactly what that means we're not sure of yet. It just seems to be a space for the students to gather, which is what this space is. And I think you'll always have staff because you'll always have people needing some kind of help and looking for that help. But if I understand their plan right, it would be more like when you go in the store, and everything is self-checkout. And things like that where you'll have people there but a lot of it will be self. We'll have to see what the changes actually are.

Q: *I think I had explained it, and maybe Professor Kinsella also explained it. Kinsella's very interested in the library, of course, and he wants to just compile a book of the library as it is at the present, talk about the past, think to the future, and featuring interviews with different people. Is there anything you would want to be taken away from that? Is there something you would want to say or something that you feel is important someone can take away from reading an interview with you, quotes of stuff that you've said, or anything really important that you wish somebody who is reading about the library would know about Stockton's library?*
A: I don't think that libraries are as valued as they should be.

Q: *I agree. I hadn't been a member of my public library in quite a while and I didn't realize how many services that they offered, how many different things they had that I could take advantage of – different sites that they have that you can use, different lending services, I didn't know all that. I don't know that it gets advertised enough, but like you said it's not as valued as it should be so it doesn't get told to people as much as it should. Hopefully that's something that can start to change for the better.*

A: Yeah, because the library's responsible for your ability to use the services provided for online research. Because those databases are maintained by the library. Like, "Oh look there's a book online." You can get that book online because of the library. You can get your journal articles and other research because of the library. You just don't realize it, and a lot of people come here because it's an area where they like to be in, or you like to study in. People like to come into that learning commons in their groups and work together, or go into a quiet area and study.

Q: Yeah, that's one of my favorite things to do, I like to find a nice little corner. When I'm here I feel like there's just a certain atmosphere where it makes it a little bit easier for me to focus on my work as opposed to if I were home with my dogs and they're making a racket and they're distracting me. But here it's easy to focus. So, things like the different websites we're using, like JSTOR and all those different journal article sites, are stuff that you guys really maintain – I don't think people appreciate that enough. Well, I think that was all of the questions. I don't want to hold up too much more of your time. I know you probably have lots of work to be doing.
A: Yes, well we always have, but now we have a lot to do anyway because we're getting ready to move out of here. So, we have a lot to do to get ready for the change.

Q: What's the timeline? Is it just going to be the end of the semester or are they kind of pushing you out a little sooner?
A: I'm not really sure. I think we were supposed to be out by May, but who knows.

Q: Yeah, there's definitely a lot to be done still for sure. Thank you so much. I appreciate you meeting with me. You've been here since 1980, so you've seen a lot of the changes that have happened, which is really interesting.
A: Yes, it has been interesting, all the changes. Like from the card catalog we went to the first computer system, which wasn't that great. It was a shared system of the library, and we went to another one, and it improved. We saw the changes from print material to a majority online, lots of databases that the library invests in for the different areas of study for the students. So, we've seen a lot of changes. But change is just natural. Everything changes.

Interviewed by Nicole Lanzoni

Microfiche machines in the Periodicals Room, before it was transitioned into the Learning Commons.

Preserving South Jersey History Through Recollections

An essay on *Early Recollections and Life of Dr. James Still*, James Still (1877, 2015)

The United States has a deep-rooted history of mistreating and separating African Americans from the White community, society's deemed superior race. Not until 1865 was slavery outlawed throughout the United States. But even then, the majority of previously enslaved African Americans had very poor prospects. Barriers against the Black community prevented its members from succeeding in the White man's world. Despite racial and financial barriers, James Still, whose parents had been enslaved, lived as a free man and became a highly successful physician in South Jersey. Thankfully, Dr. James, one of the most successful African Americans in nineteenth-century New Jersey, recorded the details of his life in his 1877 autobiography.

Stockton's South Jersey Culture & History Center republished Still's *Early Recollections and Life of Dr. James* in 2015 in order to share the life lessons of this significant man. It remains one of their best selling titles. Dr. James presents the details of his life chronologically from birth, to adulthood, to marriage, and later to his professional development as a horse-and-buggy doctor. Still focuses on his determination to become a medical practitioner and the hard work it took to maintain that position. Within his memoir he includes representative samples of cases he dealt with during his career.

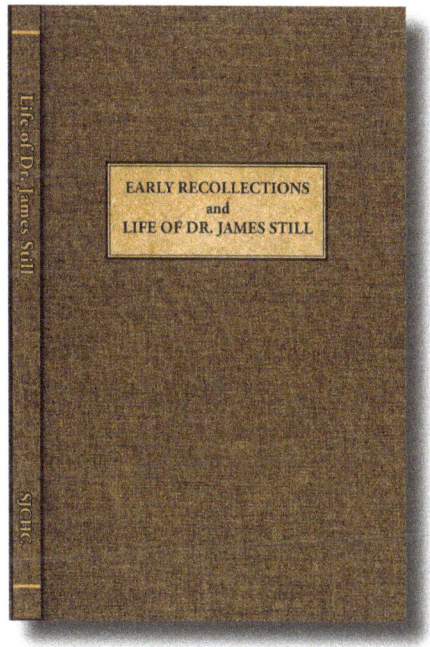

Even after his medical practice began to flourish, Still reminds his readers of the struggles he faced due to his race. In one example, he offered his medical opinion in the case of a young woman suffering from a tumor. A fellow doctor in the local community, called in for a second opinion, refered to Dr. Still using a racial slur, arguing that Still's racial background would be the cause of the woman's death (101). This patient therefore left the care of Dr. Still for the second, White doctor. Despite having a client poached in this manner, Dr. Still remained understanding and accepting; he valued his patients' ability to choose their own medical advice over his need to be in charge. Dr. Still's humble and selfless reaction toward what many would consider infuriating and racist actions is due to his deep rooted Christian faith. He declares that the "Almighty God" is just and "knows no prejudice" (102).

Throughout his memoir, Dr. Still depicts various aspects of his medical career. He especially highlights his belief in herbal remedies, specifically in regards to cancer, as surgery was the predominant treatment attempted in this period. Describing the cancerous disease spreading in a "rapid manner . . . the patient is literally destroyed by a slow and virulent poison . . . to which poor mortals are subject to" (120). Although Dr. Still performed surgical operations, he focused his attention on homeopathic methods, or "vegetable medicine." He argues that the usage of natural elements, such as "May-apple root," had been shown to have healing properties (123). Nearly 150 years ago, Dr. Still described cancer as "the very worst kind" of disease, an observation with which most, if not all, would agree. Intriguingly, the *Early Recollections and Life of Dr. James* details medicinal practices that were relatively new and evolving.

This memoir of Dr. James Still is a notable historical text that uncovers racial attitudes and scientific/medical approaches from a time long past. Dr. Still's reactions and insights retain great resonance and his life experience as a Black physician conveys meaningful lessons that remain applicable today.

Taina Altagracia

Interview with Lydia Javins

Anisah: How long ago did you retire from the Library?
Lydia: I retired roughly fifteen years ago.

Q: When you retired, was the library that you remember today's library?
A: Yes, but I was a student here before that. I started here as a student in 1986 and it was the other library. They renovated this right after I graduated and by the time I came back as a staff member it was done. So I missed the worst part of it. I picked the right three years to be gone.

Q: You were a student worker, I think you said?
A: I was a student worker downstairs in Media Services and also up here in Periodicals, which was basically the same space and they just kind of turned everything 180 degrees. It was weird; I don't know why they did that. But they got something out of it. So, yeah I was a student worker in Periodicals and also in Media Services. But, that was it.

As a staff member, I started in circulation and I moved over to become the administrative assistant for the Director and at the time I had just gotten my masters in library science and so what he did, the new director David Pinto, he turned me into his personal librarian. So I did a lot of institutional research and things like that. After six years with him, he wanted to convert a space that had been slated for the archives, but which was basically filled up with garbage that people didn't know what to do with. He wanted to turn it into a true archive. Actually, the President wanted it to be an archive because we were approaching our fortieth anniversary. So, David Pinto assigned me down there because he thought I could do it and I got the basic structure going before I had to retire.

I retired on disability; it wasn't my choice to go. I would still be here if I could. I at least got the foundations set for the new Special Collections librarian, Heather Perez, and she kicked the field goal. She's done a great job.

Anisah: I love Special Collections.
Lydia: I do too.

Anisah: It's so cool. It's so cool down there.
Lydia: It was a garbage dump originally. You would open a box and it would be garbage and then you would find something important at the bottom that deserved to be in Special collections, a map, or something. So you had to go through every box and place little stuff in the garbage, and then save. It was garbage or save. It was all sorting to begin with. After you got rid of the garbage, then you could start to fine sort the material you decided to save and I fine sorted it, me and a few student workers. We fine sorted it according to "visions," "departments," and that sort of thing all over the school. So the President's office, the Provost's office, Bursar's office, ARHU . . . and slowly but surely that material got filed into a princeton box. It got filed and labeled and we put everything in alphabetical order, so that way if you knew it might come out of NAMS you could look for NAMS and you might find it in that section.

So we were pretty rough in the beginning. But, it was better than anyone had done up until that point. Then we started to bind things, so that when the school had money – when the library had money – I'd send materials to be bound up to Bill Bearden. He was the assistant director for public services and he would tell me when there was money and I would send hand trucks of material up to him and they'd send it to the bindery. They would bring it back downstairs and we would get it on the shelves looking like a collection rather than just a lot of papers.

It was a lot of work and I always used to say it was like waltzing through wet cement. Because you are making progress so slowly and so arduously and by the end of the day you felt like "I can't keep going," but then you'd go home and rest a little bit. Then the next day you'd come back and you kept plugging away at it. You could actually see the results and that's what kept you going. If you couldn't see the results, I think you would have just collapsed.

Q: We were in Kinsella's class trying to come up with a definition of a "library" and everyone has their own definition. I think personally it has evolved over the years. What is your definition of a library?
A: Well, I have a lot of different definitions. If I had to define it on a test, I would say that it's similar to a museum, only we deal with books and other papery type things, and unlike a museum you can touch it and take it home with you. But, other than that, the whole mechanism is the same. Something comes in, it gets registered, or cataloged, and then it gets checked through a few systems and it either goes out to the shelf and or goes down where it's just there and people can find it but not on display. The process is basically the same.

My personal explanation for a library is that they are cultural institutions. I think it is important that we represent the culture, many cultures, but that there is a heavy exchange culturally. Not only does the library stay open like a museum stays open, but also there should be outside activities. Like poetry readings, stuff for younger people, stuff for older people, and crossing generations. Older people listening to younger people's music and vice versa, and people there to explain it to you so that you can understand what is going on. That's my definition of a library.

Since Stockton is an academic library, my definition doesn't really work here. But it works very well in public libraries.

Anisah: I would say it works somewhat here, what with all the cultural history that we have in here.
Lydia: They do a good job, they try to, but if you go to a public library it generates a lot more from Halloween parties, to CPR classes, to learning English as a second language, and things like that. We just don't have the staff and there is so much other stuff for students to do, we don't need to fulfill that function.

Q: Do you think the standard idea of a library has changed over the years?
A: Oh god, yes. Even what they teach in library school has changed. When I went, and it was in 1996, they used to teach something called "The History of the Book," which was how books originally were: scrolls, papyrus sleeves, right up through the printing press to nowadays. Now, they teach the internet. Which somehow doesn't feel as rewarding as I think "The History of the Book" was. They did teach the history of the internet, which was interesting. I think we spent an hour on it.

My sister and I went to library school together. We went to Stockton together, we went to library school together, and we became librarians together. We both went to Drexel. She took one look at the internet and went "That's for me! That's what I want to do." She became a web architect. I took one look at the internet and went "I'm a historian. This is the dark ages looking at us. I'm going to become a paper librarian and make sure we don't lose the paper because when this (internet) goes down, we're going to need a back-up." So I became a paper librarian and we both don't butt heads on it. We give each other the room because yes we are going into the future but as we do so we should not forget the past. We are two ends of the same spectrum.

I think libraries are being pushed into electronics too quickly and without any consideration of what they might need. I understand why they might not want to hold on to paper because of the amount of time it takes to just catalog the stuff. In paper-based libraries, you had to type out three cards for each book title. One for subject, author, and title. That took a lot of time compared to cutting and pasting now. I can see why they don't want to go backward, but some materials in paper still exist, look at Special Collections and Archives. Someone has to look at, consider, and decide "We need to keep that."

Q: Do you think paper librarians will still exist in 50 years?
A: Yes, however, it will be specialty. It won't be under the same roof and it won't be as in demand, just like archivist is not the same as librarian. We kind of restore things from the past, while librarians are always interested in bringing in the newest material because that's what people generally want. You wouldn't really go in and destroy a Van Gogh, of course, even though it's not really relevant to today. It's nice and pleasant to look at. To librarians and others it's nice to touch the paper, nice to smell the book if it's not moldy, so kind of like a museum again. It goes back to the museum comparison.

Q: You touched on a little bit of what you used to do. What were some of your other job responsibilities, besides cataloging?
A: I never cataloged. I never learned to catalog because I never wanted to do it. Most people hate it. I was afraid I'd like it and I'd get stuck with it. I never took cataloging in school. Primarily, my specialty is as a security librarian. My job was dealing with crime in the library and there is always crime in libraries. People do like to misbehave in libraries. It's different crime in different libraries. But, when I first started here I did not have my degree yet and I worked in circulation and I just checked people in and checked people out. I worked nights and weekends.

Then I moved over to the office with director David Pinto. He was very energetic. You know the character of Woody in Toy Story, he looked like Woody, he sounded like Woody, and he acted like Woody. He was a terrific leader and people just followed him. He had good ideas and I was lucky because he watched me for a while and put me on different projects – he did this with everybody – saw what people were good at it, and seemed to like doing, and then switched everyone's job responsibilities to the things that they really liked doing. So, with him I worked nights and I worked weekends. He let me develop forms for taking crime reports in the library. He had me doing institutional research like calling all the other state libraries at state schools and asking them what their archives looked like. Rowan is the only one that has an archive, besides us. Things like that.

Phone calls, developing forms, cleaning out the supply closet, and just generally whatever he needed done that I could do. Like I said I got sent downstairs to the Archives and that was work sorting papers and trying to lend structure to something that had none at all. So really to be a librarian you are basically an organizer.

Q: I remember you saying that you did not have a particular best memory, or favorite memory.
A: No. I thought about that after you emailed me and I realized that Stockton is really one long favorite memory.

Anisah: That's nice.
Lydia: We used to, especially at night, play games with each other, like, taking skittles, wrapping them in rubber bands and shooting them at Reference because there was a window and, if we could, we would bounce the skittle off the window. We used to call other Reference librarians and ask them joke reference questions, stupid things like that. You know, those are fun memories.

Q: Is there a particular academic year that you remember the most? It doesn't have to be your favorite, but just standing out the most.
A: Yeah, there is. Not for good reason, again. Something a lot of people don't know about. Let's see I started here in 1986, so it was 1987. There was a shooting here up in SOBL, well the shooting was a murder.

Anisah: Yes I do remember someone saying something about that.

Q: Do you have a favorite book or any materials here that are your favorites?
A: Favorite materials in this library? Or personal favorite materials?

Q: In the library.
A: I have an interesting story, but they're not my favorites. Nothing comes to mind right off. No, I can't think of anything. It would probably be something in Special Collections. I guess the thing that rises to the surface first is the key to Atlantic City, which was given to an amateur historian, and he donated his entire collection here. His name was William Leap and part of the Leap collection was

this box that had the key to Atlantic City in it. I had never seen a key to a city and had thought it was just some made up stuff, but no they actually exist. I had always thought that was interesting.

The thing I enjoyed working on the most was . . . This is the funny thing I discovered working in archiving. When you start doing something, whether it's business, school, or a personal project, you don't have time to keep track of progress. You are so busy trying to make it happen that nobody pays attention to what is going on around you until you finally sit back. Publishing my first book would be a good example for you. So, for the first seven years of Stockton no one really kept pictures, diaries, anything. We came across a box of pictures that somebody had dug up from some place. They were all slides and David Pinto had me put them in order. It was the actual building of the campus before they broke ground until after they completed the primary building, A- through N-wings, and when I became the archivist downstairs I looked at the first picture and saw the original house from the farm. It was the Lingelbach farm and it was the original house that had sat on this property. You could see it in the background behind the construction trailer. I was trying to get it enlarged right before I had to leave. I don't know if it ever made it in reality but that was such a cool thing to find. It was a little white house. If you don't know who the Lingelbach family is, Ethel Noyes was a Lingelbach. It was an old rather distinguished family and this was their hog farm where we sit. Lake Fred was a cranberry bog in the early 1900s. Those who came before shaped a lot of what the college is. So, that house is pretty special if you look at it that way.

Anisah: That's interesting. A cranberry bog . . .
Lydia: What we call the "Dark Path" was actually an equipment path that they put in. They hammered, pile drove pine logs into what was a lake, or a large stream to back up Lake Fred and created Lower Lake. That's now that Dark Path, but that's how they used to bring equipment across the lake.

Anisah: There is so much history. You would think . . . was it the 1970s? It doesn't seem like that much time, the '70s until now.
Lydia: It's really not.

Anisah: The amount of history just makes it seem like 200 years or something.
Lydia: And you wonder what it's going to be like in 200 years.

Stockton in 1971, before A- through D-wings were completed. See the Lingelbach farm at the left center of this photograph. Parking lots 1–3 are under construction and Atlantic City can be seen in the distance.

Q: Do you have a favorite area in this whole place?
A: In the library?
Q: Yeah. Also, in Stockton?
A: Also, in Stockton. I used to hang out in K-wing in the gallery when I was a student here. Even when I was a staff member here. In the library, I always liked the light in the afternoon back in what's now Reference. In the back of the school on the middle level, it's really nice to sit back there in the wintertime when the sun is setting. It just has such a warm light. You feel, I don't know, it just makes you feel good. It's just fun to go back there and watch the sunset. So yeah, I guess I do.

Q: Can I talk about your poem?
A: Sure.

Anisah: I read your poem. Loved it.
Lydia: Thank you.

Anisah: Particularly, there is this one line that might be in the last stanza or second to last stanza. Where you are talking about your memories and you say "They honeycomb my past," I love that line.
Lydia: Thank you.

Anisah: Particularly, I love the word "honeycomb."
Lydia: It's a weird word for that, but yes. Somehow it felt right.

Q: It is. I was wondering other than it feeling right, why you chose that word?
A: Somehow – it sounds stupid – I think of how your brain stores memory. It kind of feels like a honeycomb, you know each section has its own, like a file on a computer, it has its own little file. As you get older, you add to that honeycomb. It gets harder and harder to find the file you are looking for, so you have go through alphabetically or something subject wise sometimes. But, yeah it does feel like you are putting honey in a honeycomb so that you could go back each time you want to think about it or see it in your mind. I think about Stockton a lot. I live closer now than I used to. I would come more but they made parking here so difficult that I can't just come here and park, otherwise I would come more.

Q: When did you . . . you wrote your poem after you retired?
A: Yes.

Q: How long after? Or was it immediately?
A: It wasn't immediately. My doctor forewarned me – I have chronic fatigue syndrome – I would end up on disability and roughly how long I had. So I was here for quite a number of years before it finally took me out, which meant I slept for an entire year after I stopped working. Literally, I lost an entire year. I didn't even know it had happened. Two years after that, I felt good enough to start working on a chapbook of poems about South Jersey, specifically Little Egg Harbor. Because I worked in Special Collections and noticed that we had all sorts of bizarre books on Elmer, and other towns that you never hear of. Who writes poetry on Elmer? I realized that Little Egg Harbor, there

was nothing on it. It wasn't always going to be the way it was right then, it was going to change and get more crowded. It's not going to be as an environmentally pleasant place as it was when I wrote that chapbook. So, I started writing a book on Little Egg Harbor and I don't know why I wrote a poem on Stockton to put in there. After I put the whole thing together I realized it didn't belong. It's not really publishable because no one knows Stockton and then I realized the poem really belongs to Stockton. When Kinsella asked about poetry, I thought well this poem is for you. I wrote it for me, but it belongs to you guys. So that's when I gave it to him. I don't know what he'll do with it.

Q: I am going to ask my last question. With the renovation happening, is there anything you would like to see carried over into this new library? It could be a physical thing or just an attitude or anything like that.
A: I would like to see the art carried over to the new library, specifically that sculpture that sits in the exedra. I like that thing, the Plum and Rose, I always have. One of my jobs was finding the artist because it broke down and we had to repair it. When I was in the office, I tracked him down and called him up. "Turn on the on button. There is a little fan in there, just click it on and it will work." And it did. I would like to see that carried over. The Salvador Dalís that are on the wall around it, they're originals. They should get some airtime too. And the map you like so much.

Anisah: I wonder where they are going to display all this. I haven't really looked at the renderings of everything, but I feel like there is space for a lot more art. There was one more thing I was curious about. You said your sister worked with you here?
Lydia: Yes and no. She worked TES in Reference. She was a reference librarian here on Saturdays for like a year. But, she went to school with me here too. So, it was like coming home for her too.

Q: What's the age difference between you two?
A: Not much. Thirteen months.

Anisah: My sister and I are nine months apart.
Lydia: People look at you really weird when you are that close. It seems easier to just say, "We're twins."

Anisah: That is all the questions I have. Thank you.   Interviewed by Anisah Dean

Stockton is my Home
by Lydia M. Javins

Stockton is my home,
though it's not where I live.
I've spent twenty-two years here.
Its very foundation has soaked into my being,
my soul's ensconced by its walls.
I see my face, a floating reflection,
that has become encased in its glass.

Toward the end,
I told myself
to make visual memories
of its white, sharp-edged corners
superimposed against the
chicory-blue fall sky.
Of oaken leaves held captive by
the dusky, grey of their rumpled bark,
as nodding ladies' tresses bloom
against the lips of Lower Lake.

Memories . . .
memories of students pushing
against frigid, lakeborne winds,
or lounging, long and lizard-like
in the subtle, warming, cult of May.
These are the snap shots garnered,
fixed, emblazoned within my mind.
Cherished images, phantasms,
pressed in amber.

Now that I am gone.
These memories maintain my being.
They are the competency of my future.
They honeycomb my past.
They nourish and sustain my Self.

. . . Because,
Stockton is my home,
but it's not where I live –
not physically.

Spend enough time in the library and you become familiar with the regulars. Members of the library community have not always been limited to students and library staff. For years Precious (2006–2023) lived on and under the G-wing seating area outside the library. She was fed and protected by many on campus. She was loved by all.

Seasons: Deep, Cool Persistence In The Present

A second essay on *Seasons*, Dallas Lore Sharp (1915, 2014)

Nature asks to be known. Its riches, accessible firsthand by sight and sound among the other senses, can also be experienced through reading. By paying careful attention to nature's sensory delights, Dallas Lore Sharp conveys the outdoor world brilliantly in *Seasons*, describing life in the Pine Barrens as he experienced it.

Delving into each season, Sharp highlights various elements a reader *ought to* see and hear, Where forever *deep* and *cool* woods prevail, the hearts of those who care to experience their wonders are instantly won. From the whistling language of insects, to the desolate yet spirited haze of frost on grass – enumerable natural settings stimulate the senses. Summer, Autumn, and Winter each convey the recurring language of nature, but it is Spring, the birth time, where the life and language of the woods begin.

Springtime does not command. Instead, the birds that hatch into a freeze and flourish into warm daylit skies instill their image naturally, or perhaps maternally. As days lengthen and uplift, various birds mirror the mother-principle (a hardwired skill, an apparent condition of all life to culminate in succession). They even wade into mother-passion (an acquired skill, the condition of unconditional love). Sharp aptly and beautifully describes Spring as maternal. His excitement is infectious, repeated for the same birds, nests, and eggs of Spring, day after day.

Springtime does end, turning to its successor. Air grows hot, transforming into summer. It then cools, submitting to Autumn and to Winter. Despite all of this, it is as if "nothing unusual were happening to the history of the world" (53). Change is constantly underway, yet the usual *cool* and *deep* of the woods remains. Summer is relished; Autumn is preparation; Winter is a somber, an empty echo at what appears an end. But even bitter cold is not without birds tending to their nests. They heed their invitation to fly, and come Spring they will return. Springtime and birds, classic symbols of freedom as Sharp portrays them, convey hope and wonder to readers all year.

The other seasons are not without their enticements. To see and hear Summer is to prosper; to see and hear Autumn is to prepare for Winter. Winter woods – bruised black and blue – now fit their tokened *deep* and *cool* more than anytime else. The animals have not fought against its brutal onset; rather, they acknowledge its inevitability and accept this time of quiet. Perhaps this is not unlike what the rest of us *ought* to do.

Springtime returns. One begins again in the same place. The woods maintain their ethereal quality, to not be stuck in the past or the future, but to truly engage with the here and now. A certain songbird, a Phoebe, teaches this to Sharp, and he recounts it to us: "It's what you are! Not what you do, but how you do it!" (27). The appearance of isolation here truly does deceive. The Phoebe is right: *how* your seasons are spent tells well *what you are*. For Sharp, there seems no stronger peace than to reside in and to connect with the seasonal rhythms of the natural world. The same is surely true for you and me, if only we allow ourselves the opportunity.

Shannon McGivney

Interview with Heather Perez, Special Collections Librarian

Heather, the Special Collections Librarian, gives us some insight on her position at Stockton and how she envisions the new library.

Danielle: Best memories or stories about the Stockton library?
Heather: My favorite memories are seeing the light go on in students' eyes as they make connections or come to a realization. Whether I'm working with a student to find resources for their papers and research projects or I'm introducing an intern to Special Collections, I love that moment when a student "gets it" and understands how essential information is (and, by extension, how important the library is for finding that information).

Q: What is your favorite book or books found in our library (and why)?
A: It would have to be the Atlantic City history section (F144.A8). I'm fascinated by Atlantic City history and local history. Some favorites of mine are *The Northside* by Nelson Johnson, *Boardwalk Empire*, also by Johnson, and *The Last Good Time* by Jonathan Van Meter.

Q: What is your definition of a library?
A: As a place, the library is a location to gather and be surrounded by information, as well as a place to ask for help finding and parsing that information. As a concept, it's where information is gathered and stored and accessed – whether in a physical building or in an online environment.

Q: What do you hope remains of the old library? What aspect would you miss?
A: I hope the students come back! We've just started to recover from the pandemic – lots of students found other places/ways to study for a number of years and our book circulation went way down, as well as the questions we answered for students. Now though, the current students seem to be using the library more than ever. I'm concerned that if the building is closed and the study space in the temporary library location is limited, that students will find other places/ways to study and access information and won't need/want to use the new library spaces.

Q: What do you think is the most important aspect of the library?
A: Can I pick two? I would say the people and the resources. The people who work in the library are devoted to their jobs and to helping students. Whether it's someone at the Circulation desk checking out things or a librarian teaching a class or our Administration fighting for the money to buy resources, we are all passionate about our jobs. We have amazing resources at Stockton – databases, books, videos, Special Collections. There's so much information that no one could ever exhaust it all. And what we don't have, our incredible people in Interlibrary Loan go out of their way to bring it to you from another library.

Q: Why did you come to work at Stockton's library?
A: I was working as the archivist at the Atlantic City Free Public Library. Because of some administrative changes, they moved me to management, and I wasn't working with the special collections anymore. I knew that wasn't what I wanted, so I started to look around and apply to other jobs from Virginia to Hawaii, and then, lo and behold, the position for Special Collections Librarian opened up right here! I'm so glad I get to stay in the area AND work with special collections. A bonus for me is that I also get to work with students, which I didn't get to do much at the public library.

Q: How does technology impact your job in the library?
A: Technology is very important to my job. To publicize our Special Collections, I create a webpage for each collection, I create a library catalog entry for each collection, and many times, we digitize parts of the collection and put them online. I'm always on the computer, whether it's email, doing research, writing up finding aids, or participating in Zoom calls. In regards to emerging technologies (AI, etc.), I think that it will be very hard for them to replace my job, in particular, because a machine isn't going to be able to sort through paper documents and make sense of them, organize them, and synthesize the information into finding aids, catalog records, and webpages.

Q: What does a librarian do? What do you do in the library?
A: Librarians have many different roles and job titles, even here at Stockton. In general, librarians collect, organize, and provide access to information. I wear a number of different hats here in

the Stockton library. As a subject liaison librarian, I'm the contact for ten different academic programs. I teach library sessions for them, I meet with students one-on-one to help them with research, I select books to add to the collection, I deselect books (weeding) to remove from the collection, and I compile and share statistical information about the use of the resources. As the Special Collections Librarian, I negotiate with donors who want to give their collections to us; I supervise interns and staff in working with the collections – inventory, organizing, writing finding aids, cataloging, digitizing; I work with researchers (students, staff, faculty, community visitors) to find resources that will help with their topics of interest and teach them how to use Special Collections; and I also serve as the de-facto University Archivist, which means that I frequently have to do a deep-dive into the archives to answer questions about university history and precedent.

Q: What do you see as the future of Stockton's library?
A: I see a bright, light new space that will be an amazing place for students to gather and study. I see a larger Special Collections with a Reading Room/classroom that will accommodate full classes. I see technology continuing to evolve and shape how our campus uses library resources – more digital, less paper, but at the same time, the library as a place is still needed and used because the technology instruction is still needed and that gap can be filled by the library.

Interviewed by Danielle Palumbo

Two views of the lower-level exedra. For years, directing students to the Special Collections reading room was easy: "Take the elevator or stairs to the lower level – don't say basement – and turn left at Mr. Pothead" (above). Later, after the contribution of Congressman Frank Lobiondo's papers, the directions became more conventional: "Left at the American flag."

To Serve and Protect

An essay on *The Outfit*, Charles "Budd" Wilson Jr. (2017)

"Police" is defined as the civil force of a national or local government responsible for the prevention and detection of crime and the maintenance of public order. A well trained police force along with respectful and law-abiding citizens both are needed to fashion a working society. Police units have been in existence in various forms for hundreds of years, enforcing laws and providing protection for the people and communities which they serve. Although their basic duty, protect and serve, has not changed over the years, the way police get around, communicate with others, and live has changed dramatically. *The Outfit* (2017), recollections of Trooper C. I. "Budd" Wilson, tells the story of his life and time serving New Jersey as a police officer.

Charles I. Wilson was a New Jersey State trooper in the 1920s. After attending the 50th reunion of the Battle of Gettysburg as a Boy Scout in 1913, Wilson realized that he wanted to become a police officer. The examination to enter training to be a New Jersey State trooper has never been easy and Wilson had to apply twice before he was accepted. He passed a series of physical and mental tests in order to join the force and started his career stationed at Chatsworth, Burlington County. His first state issued vehicle was a horse. During his four-year career with the state police, he rose in rank from Trooper to Corporal to Acting Sergeant-in-Charge. Wilson then took a leave of absence to join the police force on the newly constructed Delaware River Bridge where he stayed for the next forty-six years, eventually serving as Captain of Police on the Delaware River Bridge (later to be renamed the Benjamin Franklin Bridge).

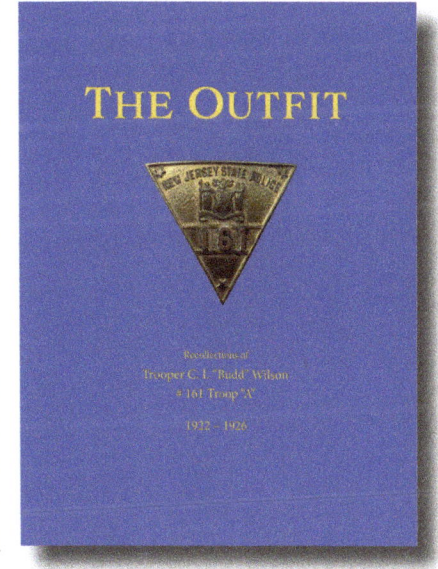

Citizens who want to become police officers today must also attend several interviews, undergo background checks, and pass a series of psychiatric tests to ensure they are mentally fit before attending a police academy. South Jersey has various academies in which recruits can enroll, depending on the township they will serve. During the academy, the mental and physical strengths of recruits are put to the test. They learn the laws they must enforce, how to communicate with community members whom they serve, and appropriate methods to protect themselves and others. The training to become a police officer is rigorous and taxing, both mentally and physically. This brief tract describing the career of Budd Wilson Sr. captures a moment in history, but also clearly depicts the life of a determined man who knew he wanted to serve and protect the lives of others.

Emma Marsico

The South Jersey History and Archeology Collection of Charles "Budd" Wilson Jr. preserves a wealth of photographs, archaeological research, and the correspondence of Emma Van Sant Moore with Hollis Koster, a noted local botanist. To the right is a draft of Van Sant Moore's poem "Fools Gold," dated February 10, 1946.

Below is Budd Wilson Sr. astride his first state issued vehicle. The photograph is preserved in his son's collection.

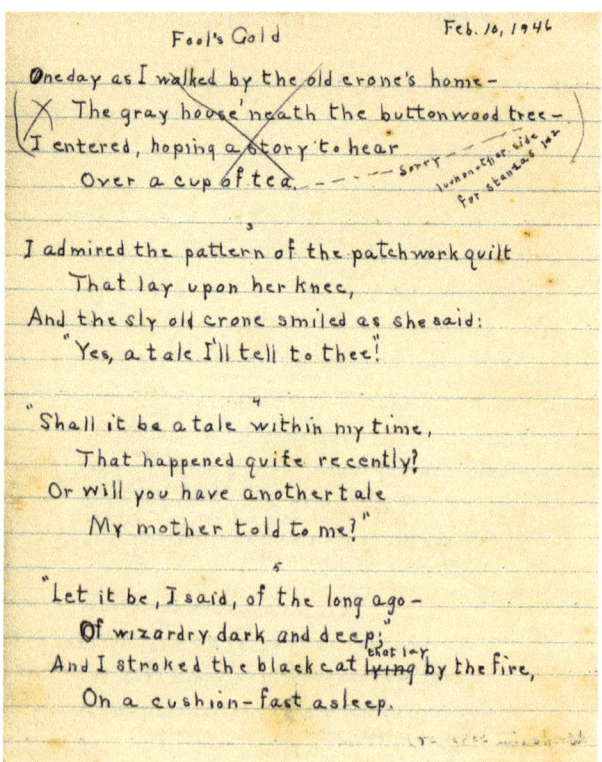

Interview with Nicole Barnabei, Technical Library Assistant

In the middle of February 2024, I sat down with technical Library Assistant Nicole Barnabei to find out what she thought about the library's transition and renovation. We had been hearing that the library was getting rid of the majority of their books and we wanted to find out more. Nicole was quick to put this rumor to rest. She said that of course they would be weeding outdated and duplicate books, but the library would definitely be keeping what was necessary. She pointed out that many books, especially those in Special Collections, remain in copyright and cannot become part of the digital collection.

We talked a lot about ways that the library has changed and what Nicole's vision for the future of the library might be. She had a lot to say about how kids and young adults learn in different ways than we did in the 1980s and 1990s and how the new library and all learning institutions need to reflect those changes. I loved her idea that the library is a "central hub for learning" and how she would like to see other departments incorporated into the library, such as the tutoring center. Nicole feels confident that as a central hub for learning, libraries will never be a thing of the past. A library isn't just about accessing information but about understanding and appraising that information – and librarians are a key component in that task.

Nicole also talked about how the Stockton library has changed over the years that she has worked there. She started at the reference desk in the early 2000s when her children were small and she wanted to work evenings and weekends. Her background had been in the legal field as a paralegal. While this job first allowed her to stay home during the day with her children, she quickly decided to pursue her masters degree in library and information sciences from San Jose State University. One of the biggest changes Nicole noted was the noise level. When she was a college student, and when she began working at Stockton, the library was a silent place to study. There was no learning commons. As the learning commons came into being and grew in popularity, so did the noise level. Nicole did not think this was a bad thing – the learning commons is a place for students to collaborate, and plenty of quiet study spaces remain.

When I asked Nicole about the ways technology influences her job, the conversation turned to AI and how it affects the library and university. She said it is still something new and we don't really know how it will impact us going forward. Librarians, however, have already seen some effects on the literature and journals they receive.

We also discussed Covid-19 and how that changed the library. Nicole said quite a few people did not return to work after the Covid-19 pandemic and that it has deeply affected the library and the jobs that library workers perform. While Covid-19 allowed for more remote access to many library and university services, it precipitated a loss in foot traffic. Only now are the librarians finally seeing people trickle back in to use the library in other ways.

Interviewed by Amanda Brady

Growing Together

An essay on *The Out of Doors Club*, Samuel Scoville Jr. (1919, 2018)

In our modern society where family members seem increasingly disconnected from one another, whether due to busy schedules, increased use of technology for entertainment, or just plain lack of common interests, Samuel Scoville Jr. offers readers a chance to meet a very tight-knit family. Though dating back to the first quarter of the twentieth century, this entertaining work strongly suggests that families are not destined to end up disconnected. *The Out of Doors Club* includes twenty adventures that follow the Band, five children and their fearless Captain (a.k.a their father), as they explore the Pine Barrens of New Jersey. From wintertime ice skating to springtime scavenger hunts, there is nothing that this group doesn't get up to together in the great outdoors.

The spirit of adventure and family is alive and well within these tales. While following along, readers feel as though they too are part of the Band. We get the chance to go on river adventures to find Jason's Golden Fleece (or at least the Band's version) and to explore haunted ghost towns. There seem to be no limits to what can be explored and learned in the Pine Barrens.

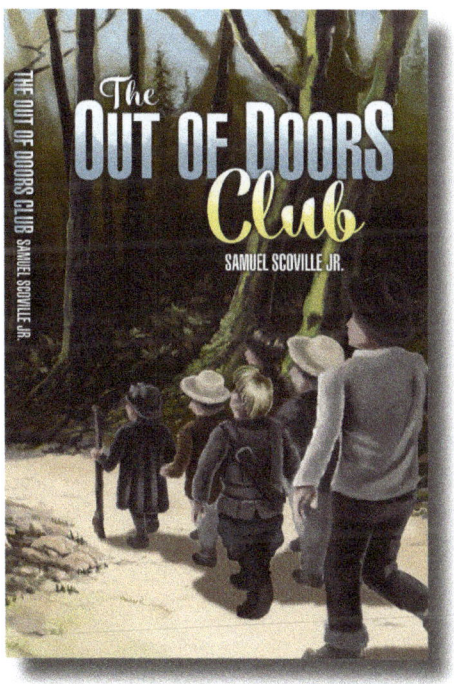

Scoville illustrates that even with busy schedules, work, and school, a family still can make time for one another. Readers feel the Band's excitement whenever the Captain comes home early from his law practice to spend the day adventuring with his children or when the Captain takes his family to their cabin on Rancocas Creek trekking through the forest together.

Scoville portrays realistic family dynamics and emotional moments relatable to any reader who grew up with siblings. Readers feel the fear radiating off of Mother and the Captain when they can't locate young Alice in the forest as well as the excitement of the children when showing off to their parents their knowledge of nature. Each chapter is filled with familial lessons that can apply to us all.

Scoville made this indoor-loving Jersey girl desire to go visit the nearest state park with her family just to witness even a sliver of the beauty of nature the Band experienced – no mean feat. Some may claim that there are no important discoveries to be made in the great outdoors, at least none that could bring families closer together, but the Captain would beg to differ: "The world is full of wonderful adventures for those who look for them" (113).

The Out of Doors Club, at first glance, is autobiographical, and each detailed adventure has a ring of authenticity. But upon further inspection, some facts do not follow the details of the Scoville's life. One of the biggest differences is that the eldest child, with an active role in nearly every story, could not have been present as described since he died at the age of two. The fact doesn't mar the impact of the story; instead, this discrepancy makes the adventures of the Band all the more fantastical and memorable. Scoville imagines his family as it could have been: his son remains with the family in spirit. Like this son, readers of Scoville's book embark on these family adventures in spirit. We too feel as though we are part of the Band.

Gianna Trematerra

Interview with Eric Jeitner, User Experience Librarian

Robert: I've got seven questions for you all right? Seven bullet points. The first one I wanted to discuss has two parts: what does the librarian do and then what do you specifically do in the Library?
Eric: Okay, so broadly librarians . . . My answer will oversimplify it a little bit. I'm painting with a very broad brush.

Librarians typically fall into one of two categories. We're either very public-facing, and those librarians are often doing things with access, so we're helping to connect students with resources. What's the word I'm looking for? Research support, academic support – we do a lot of instruction so it's a lot of facing the student and faculty community on campus. Lots of outreach and lots of academic support is probably the best way to frame it briefly. The other big chunk of library work is acting as a bridge between the library and specific academic programs. There are a handful of programs on campus that I am the Subject Librarian for: Business Administration, Business Studies, Communication Studies, Counseling, Digital Studies, Esports Management, Finance, Literature, and the Philosophy & Religion programs. Sometimes it's something that you have an academic background in, but not always. That's just another part of that academic support. Another group of librarians are on the back end; they tend to work with technical aspects of things. They maintain the databases that you search in the library's online discovery tool. They also make and maintain library records, making everything findable. This is an entire group of people who work in the library, and if their job is going along and they're doing it well, you will probably never know that they're there. I'm grossly oversimplifying librarianship into these two partitions, but I think, for most purposes, that's a pretty decent model for librarians widely.

For me it's funny. Right now the exact title of my job is changing, but it is close enough that I can use my previous one. I am the "User Experience Librarian." So, what do I do specifically? I have three main duties. One is communicating with specific programs, doing instruction, and helping students with research support – public-facing stuff. I do a lot of instruction for GENs, and the other part that I do, and this is more on the user experience side, is any aspect of library service that helps any patron: faculty, student, alumni requests, whomever. Any service that they come into contact with, part of my job is to make sure that that service works and it works smoothly.

If there's a desk that somebody comes to, or if they're on the website using an electronic tool or our chat widget or whatever. I think about what it is like to use it and try to make it work as seamlessly as possible for people. That's the "user experience" part. The other part of my job is assessment. I am usually directly involved with anything that involves assessing something that the library is doing, to check and see whether we have done it well. You know, if we've set a goal for the library, did we meet the goal? I consider how we do the kind of self-examination that we do using different surveys. This is something that I spend a lot of time doing.

That said, I need to mention that because we're a small shop overall, there are only seven or eight librarians in total, there's a lot of overlap between some of our duties. We librarians end up working together quite often. Oftentimes I work cooperatively with the outreach librarian to complete our assessment projects. There are other ways in which the Student Success Librarian and the Outreach Librarian will work together on something like a student-facing initiative. There are all sorts of ways that the staff in the library work together. There's a lot of blurriness.

Q: *This is perfect. Since you brought up facing users, how does technology impact your job in the library specifically?*
A: Technology impacts every person's job that works in the library. We each engage heavily on a daily basis with technology. For me specifically, a lot of the assessment-related projects that I do are often about either setting up things like a usability study or a focus group or something like this in order to collect data. In the end, I end up having to collect, store, analyze, and pull together the data related to whatever we're assessing. That is a very big way that I interact with technology. In an instructional situation, where I'll do a library session for a class, it would be very difficult to do without technology. We are often showing students effective ways to determine credibility for a potential source, or we talk about Wikipedia and how it functions as an information tool, and how everything we have is either based on the Web or interacts and relates in some way to tech or the Internet. So almost every aspect of the library and its work is touched by technology.

Q: *How different would your job be if we weren't using technology?*
A: It would look almost entirely different. "Access" is the only through line for ways that a librarian's job has evolved historically. This, I think, is one of the few things that has not changed since medieval times. In older times, during non-digital and non-technological points in history, we've often been about collecting and preserving and storing information, and over time, that's really shifted to what I think we do now, which is mostly focused on helping to make the connection,

like helping people find useful materials, and then once they've found them, how to work with them. How do you know it's the best thing for your needs, how to evaluate it, and then work with it? That's really where the big focus of library work has gone. In a nutshell, it's less about preserving and it's more about creating access to information and evaluating the information once you access it.

Q: *That makes sense. With all this talk about libraries and how they have drastically changed, you spoke about access and how that has changed. Is there a specific definition you would have for a library now?*
A: Oh boy, that's tricky because the scope of what a library could be defined as has gotten so much wider. I would even say it has widened within the course of the past ten to fifteen years, for sure. It used to be that a librarian would think about gathering and storing knowledge. Now it is less about gathering the knowledge and more about finding it, evaluating it, and then doing something with it. Librarianship is a lot more active and kinetic, more dynamic. The approach is more like, "Okay we've got all this stuff. What do we do with it and what is the most effective way of using it academically?" I'll try to answer in a concise way. I think of a library as a space, and I'll leave that broad – virtual, physical, whatever it is – it is a space where someone can work with information in a dynamic way to reach a certain academic goal. I guess that's it in one sentence.

Q: *Since the library is getting changed a lot, what do you hope remains of the old library and is there any specific aspect of the library or place that you will miss?*
A: So, for the first question, my colleagues and I in the public services unit try very hard to be in a location that is accessible to students – where students can find us. It is debatable currently how much we have succeeded because we're in this little grouping of rooms. How many people know we're here? I'm not really sure. We have tried to be present, visible, and findable – accessible – just like the information stored within the library. It is extremely important that accessibility stays the same, and to get better. More people need to know where we are in order to take advantage of our help. That accessibility is what I hope stays the same. I hope that the renovated library is still considered a useful place for students. I know that a lot of students like the ability to study here: they can come here and find a place that they can sit and study and be left alone. There is utility for students that they find here, and I hope that always stays the same.

Q: Do you think that the library will change from a study and quiet area to more of a communal area?
A: With technology growing in importance, it's funny. Some of the research work that I have done in conjunction with another librarian has been to study and publish on silence and the physical space and quiet in libraries. As much as that seems like a very old-fashioned way of thinking about it, you would be amazed that when you ask students on this campus what they find useful about the library, there is a 50/50 split. Half of the people want an active, dynamic space that they can come to to do group work, where they can work on projects, and so on. And the other half wants a space where they can sit in absolute silence and be left alone. I think that the ideal library caters to both of those needs by necessity. If you privilege one too much over the other you are going to be left with a significant body of people on campus that are not happy and they won't find usefulness in your space, or in your library. So, I embrace making this place more dynamic and more active, but with the caveat that it's extremely important that we earmark space for quiet study because there are many students who are looking for that very specifically.

Q: With this whole place getting renovated, what are some of your best memories or stories that you have?
A: Oh boy. Wow, Thank you. I haven't – I mean I've been here for a long while but I guess compared to some folks, like, I mean jeez, I don't know how long Tom has been here but like way longer than me. I feel that there have been a lot of people who have been at Stockton for a really long time. I've just hit the ten-year mark. So for me – ask me the question – what's the question again?

Q: The best memories or stories that you have. It doesn't even have to be one of your stories, but just a story you might know.
A: Honestly, some of the best memories that I have involve teaching my classes. I also enjoy teaching library sessions. Some of my best memories are in a classroom doing a library session and the instructor is really engaged. It's as though the instructor and I are co-teaching the class. That doesn't happen all the time, but when it does, it's like chef's kiss. It feels great and the students get really engaged and they are asking questions – that feels fantastic. It sounds a little corny or maybe like a fake answer but that's honestly one of the first things that comes to mind. Also, and this is pretty essential, I like the people that I work with here. I do not think that I would have found enough enjoyment to keep me here as long as I have been without finding other people that I enjoy working with.

Q: I completely understand – especially once you finally get a group going. I feel a lot of students have taken the "be silent in class" a little too literally nowadays, so I can definitely understand why those are some of your best memories.
A: On a side note, I will throw this in. It's related to student engagement, but not actually part of the library answer. I don't often get a chance to tell any of your cohorts this, but the semester that you were in class with me was amazing [Robert V. took *Role-Playing Games* with Jeitner in 2020]. It was the Covid year when everybody was online. Without a doubt, the dynamic, the group chemistry, and the level of engagement and investment from everybody who was in that class, I don't know that I have had another since then that has had that same kind of level. I feel like that group of you all were different in a very special way that I have not encountered since.

Q: I think one day we even, I think, we dressed up? For Halloween, a few of us surprised you on Zoom when we dressed as our RPG characters and such.
A: I don't know whether it was just the particular personalities that got thrown together. I have had other classes since then where, oh, a handful of people really seem to jell well or one of the groups really seems to hit it off. But as a whole your class was different and it was just something that I have not had.
 I think a lot of us also had, we had experience in the systems.
 Oof, boy, right, so we were definitely off to a good start heading into the class for sure and that, I think that does help. There's often, typically, between two-thirds and three-quarters of the people thinking, "What's this class about?" That kind of thing.

Q: They're probably thinking it's gonna be like Monopoly.
A: Right, right, anyway that was just a little side note.

Q: Since you brought up how your friends have helped you stay here, this last question will be perfect. Why did you originally come to work at the Stockton Library and why now do you continue to work here?
A: Oh, you know what, it's funny. I am going to give the most unexpected answer for the first part. It is going to sound very mercenary. When I was working at another library as a librarian, I liked where I worked. I liked my co-workers decently enough. It was convenient, it was close-ish

to where I lived, which Stockton is not. But I was paid very little at that institute. Between student loans and overall finances and everything, I basically could not work there on that salary. I started applying for other jobs. And I took this, in spite of it being a hike from where I live in Philly. So in spite of it being an hour commute each way, I initially took it because the state of New Jersey Higher Ed system pays well and it was enough that even considering the cost and the tolls and everything I was still making considerably more than I was at my other job and I was like, "Well, I'll do this and, you know, help my student loans all level out, and then I'll go closer back to home again, and see if I can find something," and yet here I am. It has been ten years and that has never happened. So, I came for the pay, a salary, and then stuck around for something else.

Interviewed by Robert Vassallo

Gratitude

An essay on *Back to the Land: Alliance Colony to the Ozarks in Four Generations*, Ruth Weinstein (2020)

> "Once I understood what a story was, strands of my mother's family history in the old country and their emigration to the United States were well braided into my own idea of who I was and where I belonged in the world."

Ruth Weinstein may have spent her early years wondering where she belonged in the world, but as she wrote her memoir *Back to the Land* (2020), she had a sure sense of where she came from and where she was going. She had no doubt where she belonged in the world.

Weinstein's forebears were some of the first to become involved in the back to the land movement of the nineteenth century. They were Jews, escaping the oppression and pogroms of Russia, who hoped to find a better life farming in South Jersey. They were early participants in an agrarian cycle that has recurred through the years – in the late nineteenth century, the 1930s, the 1960s and 1970s and now again in the 2020s. Such movements are identifiable by their anti-modern, communal ideals, with adherents who strongly believed in the dignity of working with one's hands.

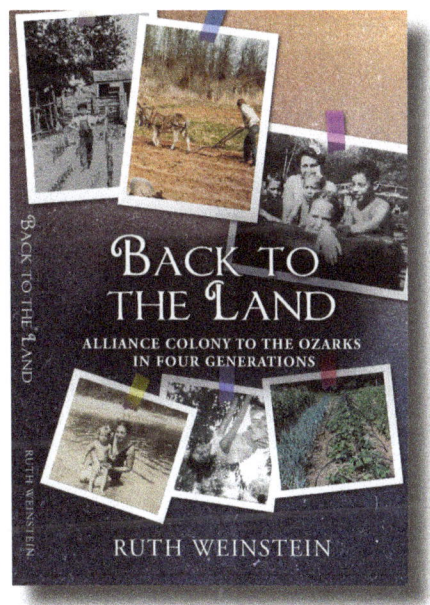

John Levin, Weinstein's grandfather whom she refers to as Pop, was influenced by *Am Olam* agrarian idealists of the late nineteenth century. Weinstein and her husband Joe went back to the land in the 1970s, farming to this day on forty acres in the Ozark mountains.

While agrarian movements are not exclusively Jewish, Weinstein's views are in sync with those of Noah Phillips, who writes that many young Jews "have embraced the farmstead as the twenty-first century's answer to the synagogue or Jewish community center, reflecting the intersection of Jewish values, environmental sustainability and social justice. Climate change, the costs of urban living and the perennial desire to reconnect with nature have all contributed to the wave" ("A New Generation of Jewish Farmers Returns to the Land"). The reasons for pursuing an agrarian life have changed somewhat since the nineteenth century, but the attraction remains.

For some, perhaps many, nostalgia is an important and appealing aspect of such movements. In *Back to the Land*, Weinstein longs for her ancestral home and traditions steeped in the soil. Although she claims to be "wary of romanticizing" her wholesome childhood and her grandfather's simple way of life, in her own home she attempts to recreate Pop's entire kitchen with her sought after depression glass and her beloved pottery. Her memoir is full of rich language and connections between Weinstein's childhood spent digging worms and her current lifestyle digging a garden. Her heart is where her roots grow, both metaphorically and literally. Weinstein explores themes of innocence, growth, and independence, but the theme that she returns to time and time again is hardship. The hardships of land and family, both difficult at times, fuse into a nuanced discussion of "home."

This poignant memoir concludes with gratitude to Weinstein's ancestors who made the difficult journey to South Jersey for a "life of freedom in America" and whose example provided prototypes for her to follow as her own "free farmer on my own soil."

Amanda Brady

Interview with Jaimelyn Lombardo, Electronic Resources Coordinator

Lost Files

Presented with the question "what is a library," likely answers would describe the structure of a library, the collection of books on the shelves, and the nooks and corners populated by people engrossed in stories. When asked to define a library, Stockton alumna and current Electronic Resources Coordinator Jaimelyn Lombardo referred to a library as "a house of knowledge."

Her use of the word "house" resonates with many Stockton students, as the library has served as a second home to them. The core element that makes Stockton's library a home? – the students. As described by Lombardo, libraries are both repositories of academic information and "social centers where folks are congregating with a shared goal of learning." As Stockton transitions to a library with fewer books, one may ask: how are students going to be equipped to learn? Reflecting on her own memories, Lombardo suggested that "you don't just learn from the physical items in a library, you learn from the people who work there and others who just appreciate them." So, is it the books and the physical building that makes a library? Or is it the people?

When asked about her fondest memories of the library, the answers are personal. The Stockton library, according to Lombardo, is taking turns imitating Darth Vader voices over the intercom, cartwheel contests, students studying comfortably in their pajamas, and late night pizza deliveries during finals week. Lombardo emphasized the importance of these memories living on and how easy it is to "lose the echoes of those who have been here before us." Reflecting on this, we must ask, as Stockton begins its renovations looking toward a new and different library, how will we store these memories? Our hope is that part of these memories may be stored within this book and appreciated for generations of Stockton community members to come.

Interviewed by Brooke Armitage

Shipwrecks and Legends and Explorers, Oh My!

An essay on *Atlantic City: Its Early and Modern History*, Alexander Barrington Irvine (1868, 2013)

America has often relied on stories to sell mis-truths to its citizens. Is South Jersey, or specifically Atlantic City, any different? Some might say saltwater taffy, Frank Sinatra, the ever-popular slot machines, and the thunderous arrival of the USAF Thunderbirds over the boardwalk are the legendary stories of Atlantic City. Alexander Barrington Irvine paints a different picture of the resort town in his book *Atlantic City: Its Early & Modern History*. The 1868 original publication is the first printed history of Atlantic City. According to Irvine, there are three things tied to the biography of Atlantic City: railroad progress, shipwrecks, and Native American legends. It is clear from early on in the text that Irvine is trying to sell Atlantic City. To interest potential travelers or investors, he spins tall tales that are splashed with color and rich in imagination.

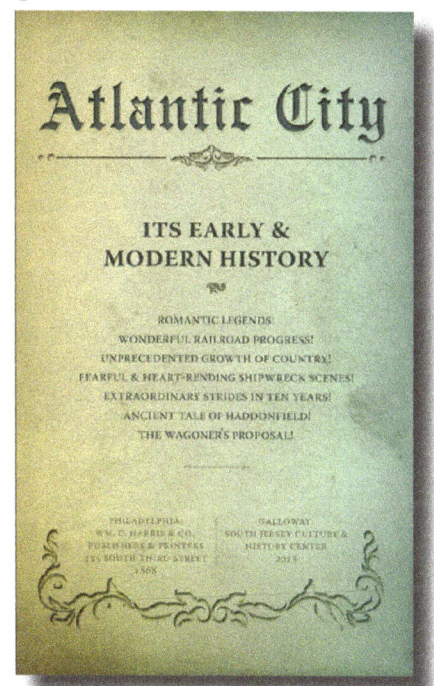

The early history of Atlantic City is somewhat murky, so Irvine fabricates a good deal of it. He lists shipwrecks off Absecon Beach with some accuracy, but his tales of the deceased passengers are often of questionable veracity. A captain named Busk wrecks his ship, GHERGE'S KHAN, and spurns offers of rescue; he instead commits suicide by plunging into the icy depths of the Atlantic Ocean. A second story describes the wife of a schooner captain who accidentally ends up overboard with her throat cut by her watch chain; a dense fog had conveniently rolled in when the wife met her demise, so neither the passengers or island witnesses are able to accurately tell her story. Irvine's infatuation with railroad progress is obvious throughout the work. He devotes important sections of *Atlantic City* to detailed discussions of the Camden and Atlantic Railroad Company. The specificity serves as a counterpoint to the pseudo historical detail.

Irvine's earliest examples of "history" in the Atlantic City area stem from the supposed manuscripts of a Portuguese explorer named Leonardo whose identity remains a mystery and is, in all likelihood, a complete fiction. This early explorer is said to have wrecked off the coast of Absecon Beach where Delaware Indians rescued him. Leonardo, we are told, spent several weeks with the tribe.

Indigenous peoples were the original residents of the American continents, so it comes as no surprise that some were occupying Absecon Island. The probability of a Portuguese explorer being rescued by the Lenape tribe is high; nevertheless, the supposed manuscripts that chronicle Leonardo's sojourn appear to be a fabrication. There is no factual evidence of a European traveler matching his description having spent time with the Lenape.

Irvine's narrative concoctions are directed at a European audience. He makes the mostly untouched land of nineteenth-century Atlantic City seem to be something of a legend. There are grief-stricken widows who lost their husbands to shipwrecks and exoticized indigenous peoples, thick with mentions of the "Great Spirit" and of demure maidens. It is worth mentioning that Irvine originally published this "history" under a pseudonym and that real history is glossed over in order to tell these tall tales. This is something too wholly familiar. It is certainly typical of South Jersey, and all of America, to craft false narratives in order to provide a "satisfactory" story.

There is an obsession that lies within the mythos of America: the creation of fake tales in order to sell an experience. Irvine's telling of the Ocean Girl tale – a love story about a beautiful, exotic native girl caught between two warriors – is a striking example. Leonardo supposedly witnessed the events of the story during his time with the tribe. Ocean Girl swoons an absurd number of times, is rescued on horseback, and a battle is fought and won for her heart. This faux legend reads as nothing but a white man's heavily fabricated dream. At the same time, Irvine pretends to debate the reason for the absence of the Delaware Indians that occurred after Leonardo's rumored departure from America. Irvine wrangles with two theories, erosion or the growing intrusion of palefaces. The answer is clear to any outside reader, yet Irvine feigns ignorance. Undoubtedly, it was the slow takeover of "settlers."

Anisah Dean

Interview with Luke O'Connor

When it comes to a large and significant University project, such as a library renovation, it is beneficial to learn students' opinions and perspectives. Enter Luke O'Connor. Luke is a senior at Stockton University who is obtaining a degree in business with a minor in information systems. Something that sets Luke apart from other students is the fact that he is heavily involved with the library renovation process.

From a young age, Luke has had a special place in his heart for libraries. In 2023, he embarked on a project, alongside library staff member Jessica Mortorano, to visit other university libraries to discover what makes them special and to determine how Stockton's library ranks in comparison. It became apparent that the Stockton library is lacking in services to students. It is outdated in technology and lacks modern spaces for students to work together.

Despite completing research on university libraries in our area, Luke didn't expect his research to be useful when it came time to plan Stockton's library renovation. Nevertheless, he has become heavily involved in presenting his research to faculty, library staff, board members, and architects so that they can see what our neighboring universities offer their students. Now, Luke helps to represent the voices of the students to help the staff decide what changes should be made.

When asked what he hopes to see from the renovations, Luke states that he would love to see more twenty-first-century technology incorporated into the library, such as data walls, 360-projection immersion rooms, and audio/video recording studios. He would love to see more modular spaces where students can adapt the space and the furniture to their needs.

As a student, I feel reassured knowing that Luke is putting thought and time into sharing his feedback with the people involved in the renovation process. I know that with Luke and Jess at the forefront of the renovations, the Stockton library will rank among the best libraries in our area at the end of the current renovation.

Interviewed by Gianna Trematerra

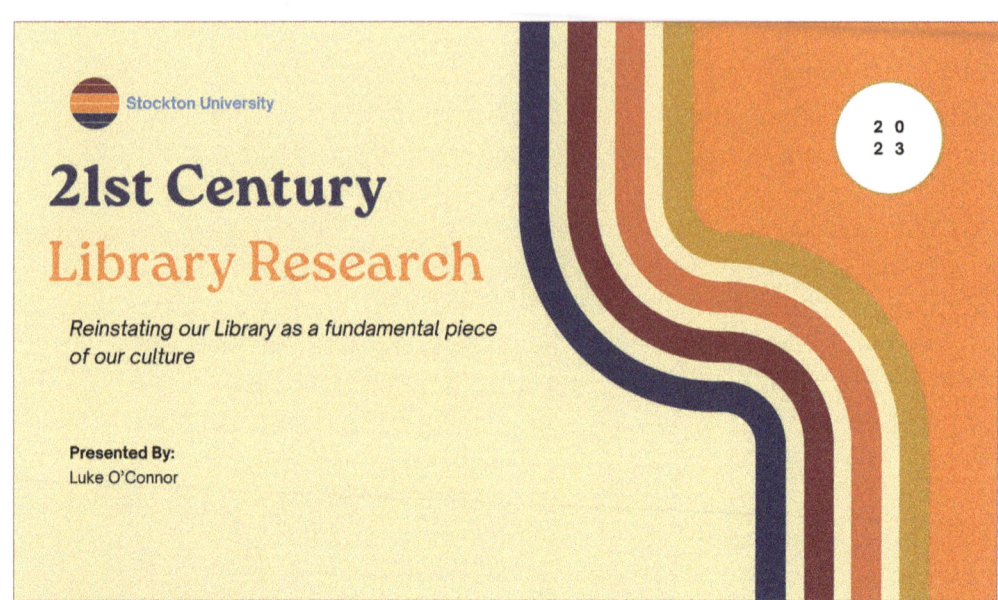

Libraries

Stages of Transformation:

1. <u>Traditional Collections:</u> Libraries started as repositories of physical books and manuscripts, serving as quiet spaces for reading and research.
2. <u>Digital Revolution:</u> With the advent of the digital age, libraries embraced online databases, digital archives, and other digital resources while still maintaining physical collections.
3. <u>21st-Century Shift:</u> Currently, libraries are in their next stage of evolution, blending traditional and digital elements to create dynamic learning environments.

Project
✦✦✦ Research

12 institutions were visited and assessed, with self guided tours

- Drexel University
- Kean University
- Monmouth University
- Princeton University
- Ramapo College
- Rider University
- Rowan University
- Rutgers University
- St. Joseph's University
- Temple University
- The College of New Jersey
- University of Pennsylvania

5 institutions were revisited with guided tours

- Drexel University
  - Innovation Studio
- Rutgers University
  - Digital Learning Commons
  - Hatchery Innovation Studio
- St. Joseph's University
- Temple University
- University of Pennsylvania
  - Education Commons

Spaces

Library learning spaces are essential hubs for focused study, collaboration, and academic growth. These dynamic environments transform studying into a shared journey of exploration and innovation, highlighting the enduring importance of physical spaces in the joy of learning.

Learning Commons/Collaborative
- Large open room, collaborative seating, allows noise, modular furniture/whiteboards

Study rooms
- Both large and small enclosed study spaces

Makerspace
- dedicated space for hands-on learning

Quiet Study
- dedicated quiet space for reading, study, and research

Updated Computer Lab
- Modular space, open-ended classroom, data wall

21st century Technology

Visualization Room

Future presentation technology Includes:
- Immersive projection
- Virtual Reality
- Data Walls
- Student Screen Mirroring

*Kean University's Visualization and Immersive Studio

21st century Technology

Makerspace

*Upenn's Education Commons

Makerspaces are education spaces that centers around creation learning:

In a makerspace, you can expect to find:

- 3D Printers
- Laser Cutters
- Sewing Machines
- Craft materials

21st century Technology

Modular Furniture

*Rutgers University's Hatchery Innovation Studio

This encompasses classroom structure, study space and furniture for learning:

- Furniture and partitions that allow for adjustable learning spaces
- Open-Ended classrooms
- Allow students to make the space their own

21st century Technology
Podcasting Booth and One-button Studio

These are recording booths set up for student's ease of use

- Podcast booth
    - audio recording
- One-Button Studio
    - Video recording
    - made to be plug-and-play
    - see next slide for more detail >

*The University of Arizona - CATalyst Studios

21st century Technology
One-button Studio

Welcome to the One Button Studio

- Insert your drive into the dock to begin.
- Press the button to start/stop recording.
- Remove your drive when you are finished.

Relevancy

Why should you care?

Library Evolution in the 21st Century:
- Vital institution in a world with diminishing public spaces.
- Transformed into a dynamic research center.

Adapting to the Digital Age:
- Maintaining commitment to learning spaces.
- Integration of cutting-edge technologies (VR, makerspaces).

Community and Learning Hub:
- Fosters community and education.
- Accessible space for diverse demographics.

Cultural Cornerstone and Continued Education:
- Acts as a cultural cornerstone.
- Essential for continued education in an ever-evolving world.

Warning Against Ignoring Importance:
- Vital utility empowering individuals.
- Ignoring significance risks loss of a crucial resource.

Blueprint for Continued Relevance:
- Contemporary library sets a blueprint.
- Captures 21st-century essence, ensuring ongoing relevance.

Conclusion

When applying this research to Stockton university, we can hope to see <u>some</u> of these elements in the upcoming renovation:

- Accessible outlets and electricity
- A focus on natural lighting
- Dedicated individual and group study spaces
- Updated technology and workstations
- Study rooms outfitted with updated technology
- Modular furniture
- Open-ended classrooms
- A makerspace
- A datawall
- Presentation/visualization technology
- Audio/video rooms
- A reading room

Follow the Stockton Library socials
@stocktonu_library

Laura Cranwell at work in Special Collections and Archives, 2018. In the background Heather Perez works in her office.

To Beauty and Beyond

An essay on *Beauty is Never Enough,* Elizabeth B. Alton (2021)

The mother of Stockton University, an active advocate for women's rights, and a powerful businesswoman – Elizabeth B. Alton was more than met the eye. Alton's memoir *Beauty is Never Enough* tells the inspiring story of a young woman with aspirations that many viewed as beyond her capabilities, beyond any women's capabilities for that matter. Hers is the life of a mid-twentieth-century feminist searching for equality in a predominantly patriarchal world.

Alton recounts the story of her life from girlhood to becoming a wife, mother, businesswoman, community volunteer, and eventually the driving force behind the creation of Stockton State College. Along the way she dissects conservative female standards and male chauvinist behavior, while reflecting on her life as a woman who wanted more. Stockton University's Bjork Library Special Collections is part of Alton's legacy, as following her example, it proudly preserves and champions feminist voices, allowing community members to reflect upon past ideas and to develop their own.

We might consider Alton and her memoir through the reflective lens provided by feminist and film director Greta Gerwig in the movie *Barbie* (2023). In her early teens, Alton walked the boardwalk of Atlantic City in a parade that was the precursor to the Miss America pageant. The ideals of the parade, and early pageant, would not pass current cultural muster. As an adult, Alton worked her way into the business community of Atlantic City. Much like Barbie, not only did Alton prove wrong those who doubted her business capabilities, she did so while demonstrating her humanity as a daughter and mother.

The original representation of Barbie has perhaps been willfully misconstrued, over time becoming a stereotype suggesting that there is only one *type* of woman that feminism supported. Anecdotes in Alton's memoir from her early life reflect this mindset. But a more nuanced feminist outlook is apparent as Alton traces the years of her life. Like Barbie, she came to fight for the representation of *all* women as beautiful, but more importantly, as powerful. Alton closed her life fighting for inclusivity for minority women, equal pay, and for the Miss America Pageant to turn from the male objectification of women to highlighting a fuller appreciation of women. The Miss America Pageant was Alton's Barbie Land, a world in which women were the epicenter.

Barbie was created for women, but controlled by men . . . until Greta Gerwig's recent reclamation. Gerwig reconfigured the view of Barbie back to its origins – representing all women as capable of more than beauty. Alton's efforts in support of the Miss America Pageant reflect this as well. The world in which the pageant originally existed was controlled by men who determined the standard of beauty highlighted in the event.

Both Gerwig and Alton reflect on the beauty of girlhood, using romanticed images such as pinning up curls and brushing on perfect pink blush. Both reclaim these moments, distorted as vanity, and reinforce their significance. Elizabeth B. Alton recognized moments of femininity as important and balanced them with ideals of intelligence and productivity. To Alton, beauty did not devalue womanhood, though, as her title suggests, it is never enough.

Brooke Armitage

Interview with Louise Tillstrom, Principal Library Assistant

George: Do you have any specific memories or stories about the library or within the library?
Louise: We had a lot of fun, got our work done, but had a lot of fun because we used to work the night shift. That's how I started, working nights and weekends. On weekends we took turns bringing in treats, and one of my coworkers brought in these pretzels that were garlic flavored. And on the way out she accidentally dropped them, and the library smelled like garlic for the next three days.

We had one time when a student brought a rifle in, and it was one of the martial arts wooden rifles in their bag. So the cops were called for that.

One time we smelled something burning and we called the police so they sent an officer, but the officer had a head cold, so he couldn't smell anything. It was like, alright we'll just let that one go I guess.

Q: Did you ever find out what the smell was?
A: No, they said it might be the campground coming through the windows. I said, "No that is definitely not the campgrounds (laughing)."

Q: When did you start working here at Stockton?
A: Oh, since 1997, I started as temp and then went to part time then to full time the day before 9/11, so that's how I remember when I started full time here.

Q: You have obviously spent a lot of time here . . . what are some of your favorite aspects of working in the library?
A: I think seeing the people and the students, because the students are always so appreciative of what we are doing in helping them. That, that is really nice.

Q: Specifically, as a librarian, how do you define a library, what is it for?
A: A library is really important, where the students do a lot of research. I think they grow here, develop more mature here. It's more than just a place for books.

Q: I completely agree, and obviously it is changing with the future and has changed since you have been here. What are some of the things that you hope remain; and those that change?
A: I don't think that there is too much more that can change, I mean there has been a lot of change since I started. We used to have stacks and stacks of books to put away at the end of the semester. We don't have that now because of computers. We are getting rid of a lot of books because they are not being used and they are online now. So, I guess if anything I hope that computers will get a little more advanced.

Q: Are you pro-technology? I mean obviously it has helped you out in your role here.
A: Oh yeah, but you have to have books, you can't do away with the books. I mean there are a lot of classics.

Q: Could you tell me a little bit more about what you have done here?
A: Well I started in circulation and came down here to Special Collections in 2009 and then we got the huge Munn donation. David Munn was a local historian and librarian who donated 10,000 items, and this was before we had our Special Collections Librarian, Heather Perez. So, it was me and the just retired director, who came back as a temp to help with everything, but we definitely needed a full-time curator. So, I was going through everything. We had boxes and boxes everywhere down here, it was a crazy . . . crazy amount of books, calendars, photos. A lot of things to go through. Given that I was not an archivist, I basically organized. You want to be able to find something, so you put it in alphabetical order and such. My boss also had me do inventory on the vertical files. That was a very good learning tool because then we knew what we had and what we could add. It has changed a lot, but that one donation it was like woooah. Special Collections used to be in the little room across from circulation, with one cabinet and a few dozen books. Heather has really done a lot for Special Collections.

Q: What do you see Special Collections doing for the area, obviously South Jersey? I feel that it holds so much information about the area surrounding us.
A: Well we try to get as much material on South Jersey as possible, and if we had it our way, that's all we would add to Special Collections – South Jersey history. You know sometimes donations are written up differently and we have to add things that aren't specifically South but also North Jersey.

[George introduces the topic of Miriam Moss's book, *Seasons in the Pine Barrens*.] *Q: Do you spend any time outside the library? Is there any place that you specifically connect with?*
A: Well, in our back room [of Special Collections] we have three big windows that we all look out all the time.

Q: Is keeping that connection to nature important to you as the library changes?
A: Yeah it is, it really is. On Saturdays I used to walk around the lake and take pictures. If you want to know my favorite books, I love photography books. I love taking pictures, I have a lot of pictures that I have taken of the inside and outside of the library.

Q: We begin rambling a bit but discuss mostly about how unfortunate it was that they had to take down so many trees in order to build the campus center. Louise felt that it was nice to have more nature than there is now, but understands how Stockton had to expand.
A: I remember taking a photography class. I was following a squirrel, taking photos that I thought were cute. When I got to class the teacher told me, "No animal photos!"

Q: Do we need books in this world that is so technology heavy?
A: Of course, you just have to say, "We have to keep those books!" I'd rather pick up a book to read, a story, instead of reading on a computer.

Q: Is there anything else that you may want to point out about the library?
A: I have always liked this library. Hopefully it just keeps going in a good direction. The changes I have seen have been positive. All we need now is for students to come in and be able to sit down with their laptop and plug in, make sure you have enough lighting, outlets, and an area where you can study and then have group discussion. That's the important thing.

Q: What do you think of the large study room [the commons]?
A: I think it's needed, as long as you can have your quiet areas, then of course we need areas where students can talk and collaborate.

Interviewed by George White

Quiet study on the first level of the library, the northwest corner, spring 2024.

What is the Worth of One Marsian's Word?

An essay on *A Trip to Mars*, Charles K. Landis (c. 1876, 2015)

In 1876, around the same time he was fighting off murder charges, Vineland's founder and city planner Charles K. Landis decided to begin writing *A Trip to Mars*. As Patricia Martinelli notes in her introduction, Landis was taking his shot at science fiction between Jules Verne in the 1860s and H. G. Wells in the 1900s, although his book was not published at the time of its writing. It wasn't until about a decade ago that his typescript was rediscovered at the Vineland Historical and Antiquarian Society.

While there is an ending to the book (with a "THE END"), the story seems to be unfinished or at least hurriedly concluded. Whether Landis misplaced the rest of the book or never wrote it is unknown, but the 132 pages that were found, although exceedingly interesting, are a bit chaotic. One could argue that its most intriguing aspect is the depiction of monsters, whose treatment and actions make one begin to question the integrity of the "utopian" Marsians.

The book follows an unnamed narrator and a mysterious "Count" as they learn about Mars in their preparations for a journey across the galaxy. The two travel in a ship powered by the magnetism of Mars's elements, which were dug out of the Count's personal mountain in Austria. After landing, they discover that Marsians (as Landis calls them) aren't too dissimilar from Earth's humans, although they are better in almost every way. The description of Marsian city life clearly depicts Landis' version of an ideal city, down to his in-depth description of how superior Marsians' sewers systems are. After this exploration, Landis gets into the most fascinating part of the book: Mars's so-called monsters.

These monsters are elephants that leap dozens of feet into the air, birds that lead flying chariots, and most interestingly, ape-like monsters with human level intelligence who, according to the Marsians, steal their women and children. These monsters live outside of the walls that Marsians have built to protect their cities and despite their alleged crimes, the narrator never actually sees the monsters attack unprovoked. This leads thoughtful readers to question which party is actually innocent.

The only time the narrator actually sees the ape monsters is when he, the Count, and several Marsians leave the city walls to hunt them. It is only when the narrator and his crew mates begin to attack that the monsters retaliate, and even that isn't immediate. When the narrator and the Count shoot down the first of the monsters, the survivors "[run] from one to the other, making lamentable noises" (99). They seem to *grieve* their fallen comrades before being shot themselves, and their brethren come to chase the humans only after the murders. Their compassionate reactions don't seem like the actions of monsters, causing the reader to think that perhaps the "lamentable noises" while not quite human, are not quite monstrous either.

The monsters present in *A Trip to Mars* are only monsters if we believe the Marsians. The only evidence of their crimes comes from the mouth of the men trying to kill them. Given the unfinished nature of the book, we have no way of knowing if Landis would have teased this idea out or continued along the same narrative lines. I suspect there is a reason that the book is subtitled "As Described by an Eye Witness." It is possibly connected to Landis' own murder charges at the time. As Landis was found not guilty due to temporary insanity, the ideas of perspective and truth were likely at the forefront of his mind.

The question becomes "what is the truth?" a question that Landis may have often pondered as he awaited trial. The reader is left to ask how much can we trust the Marsians' words, when what the narrator sees at best doesn't support the Marsians' narrative and even seems, at times, to contradict it. "What is a monster?" is a question that readers are left to ponder long after the conclusion of Landis's manuscript.

Sarah Coe

Interview with Joyce DeStasio, Outreach & Public Services Librarian

The Stockton Library carries out many functions. It provides tools for research and learning and serves as a place to foster community, knowledge, and the preservation of history. In this interview, Joyce DeStasio, Stockton's Outreach and Public Services Librarian, reveals what she thinks a library is, her new family connection to Special Collections, and her Stockton library origins.

When asked about how she would define a library, DeStasio stated, "I feel like there are physical and non-physical aspects to a library. It is this physical space we can be in where there is information, books, videos. It can be a place where we gather to talk to each other, where we can ask questions, but then there is also this conceptual, or non-physical, aspect because there is shared information and you don't have to physically be in a library to access it. We also have a large part of our library that is digital: everything we have in our databases and our ebooks. Even our Zoom calls to talk and share information with each other – that is part of what a library is. So to me, it's an info-sharing place, wherever that exists."

Joyce DeStasio is a more recent addition to the Stockton library faculty, but she had nothing but kind and loving words for the library's community. As a graduate student trying to plan for a future in an academic library setting, she saw Stockton as a no-brainer after a personal day with the faculty that was set up by Special Collections Librarian, Heather Perez.

DeStasio described enthusiastically, "Heather set up this entire day for me to come in and I met with everyone for an hour. I learned about all of the different aspects of being a librarian. What everyone did. I even had a chance to sit in on a library session with the students. That was a pivotal day for me in my school career. After that, every project I had to do, I was pulling on something that happened that day."

She even divulged that, "When, for my final semester, I had to do an internship, I reached out to Heather and I asked, 'Do you need any interns?' She didn't, but checked to see if Christy or Eric did, two other librarians here at the time, and they decided to take me on as an intern. I was here every Friday for the rest of the semester. This was fall 2021 and that was when I fell in love with this place. I was like 'I need to figure out how to work here.' Of course, that was a crazy time. They had let go of the library director at the time. Christy Goodnight, whom I was working with, became the interim director at that time and that left an opening in her spot as Outreach Librarian. She pulled me into that slot temporarily and I eventually got to stay on permanently."

"I guess my biggest memory was that first day as a student and arriving and how much everyone wanted to help. 'Yeah talk to me for an hour!' Those are the kind of people you want to work with. Those are the kind of the people who make me want to be here. And now that I am here, I hope I can be one of those people if students need help with something."

She even shared a funny anecdote about the formation of the Punktuations: "One of my favorite memories, more along the lines of what I think you're looking for, is while I was an intern, I had this idea for a Halloween costume. And I thought this could be a group costume, 'Let me see if anybody is interested.' The librarians barely knew me; I had only been here a couple of weeks. 'Okay,' I said, 'here's this idea – only a bunch of nerds would be happy to do this with me. I want to dress like a punk and be the 'Punktuations' and we will each be a different punctuation mark.

"I was just some intern no one knew, but I told a couple people and then they told more people, and it just became this big group thing. It was my idea. I was so proud of it. That was one of the first days where someone I work very closely with now, that was the day we met for the first time because we were both dressed up as punks. I'm an exclamation point and she's something – I don't remember. It was a great way to meet everybody, and I loved that everyone was down and everyone was happy to be a part of something. That kind of spirit is prevalent. It's something you see a lot here and we are all happy to work together. We have a lot of fun, too."

Stockton's library is also unique because of its Special Collections, which preserves the historical records of South Jersey. DeStasio shared that her family had recently donated their own historical collection to be added to the Stockton archives. "My family had a farm in the area that was started by my grandfather and his brothers in the 1930s. My dad and his partners, who are also his cousins, just sold it about a year or so ago. And we were going through all the old materials. Heather mentioned wanting a collection from a family farm, but my dad said no. I didn't know it was because he was in the process of selling the farm and couldn't give away the farm's property. But now that the sale is all said and done, he was able to donate the collection, with the blessing of the new owners, of course! So, Stockton will preserve a collection from the Atlantic Blueberry Company, my family's farm. I may be playing favorites because it's my family's, but I am really excited that we are going to have all of my grandparents' and father's family material here in the library. There are ledgers from the '40s, old property deeds, photos, and the advertising they used to do. It's a significant historical record, and it's really cool to see. I'm excited that anyone who comes to Special Collections will be able to work with that material now."

At the core of Stockton's library, says DeStasio, is a loving community and a unique archival record of South Jersey history. The library is a place for the communication of knowledge and history as well as a third space for the building of interpersonal relationships.

Interviewed by Victoria Orlowski

The Punktuations!

The unused patio on the first level of the library, facing the D-E-wing parking area, on a rainy day.

Making Your Own Way

An essay on *A Farmer's Daughter: Bluma,* Bluma Bayuk Rappoport Purmell (1981, 2022)

What instances define our lives? Is it the moment in which we burst into the world, air filling our lungs as we scream our arrival? Or is it the eulogy read at our funeral, the moments of our lives boiled down to haphazard anecdotes and trivial accomplishments? Do we have agency over how we live, or is the dash between the dates a preconceived span of time already decided by a higher power?

If we were to look at Bluma Bayuk's life as a barometer for these questions, it would be clear to see that control over who we are and what we become is firmly within our grasp. It is no secret that some of us are born with less means than others. Generational wealth, or lack thereof, tends to be a driving force in the direction our environment leads us. If you don't have the benefits of financial freedom, struggles are bound to stand as roadblocks in your way. You can either remain stuck in place or go around them. Bluma chose the latter.

As the daughter of a poor farmer, Bluma recognized seeds of opportunity even when the outcome seemed bleak. Her memoir explains how she left the family farm on a train bound for Philadelphia; "Seventy-five years ago, at the age of fifteen, I took complete responsibility for my own life. I knew that my future was in my own hands and that I was a mistress of my actions" (98). Even after she arrived in Philadelphia, and was taken advantage of by a brother who employed her with very little compensation, she searched for ways to succeed.

Bluma's childhood was defined by the choices of her parents; as a child of immigrant Russian farmers who escaped to America to save their lives, she inherited the rough and meager rewards of farm life. Growing up in Alliance, New Jersey, was never easy, but the love and devotion of her community made it worthwhile. As she looked back on her childhood, she pondered about others' opinions of her upbringing; "I wonder what Freud would have thought about my childhood. Was I brought up in an emotionally healthy environment? We had little play time, shouldering responsibilities at an age when most children were still being waited on" (17–18). Regardless of the difficulties of her upbringing, Bluma viewed both of her parents through very loving eyes. She describes her dad as kind and patient, "never raising his voice to us" (23). Other instances in her childhood also shaped who she became as an adult, the loss of her twin baby sisters being a catalyst for her venture into the medical field. Wanting to become a doctor was a personal goal for Bluma, but as a woman in the early 1900s, and a poor one at that, it was a far-fetched dream. She saw nursing school in a Jewish hospital as a way to climb the ladder, bringing her one step closer to her dream.

However, she would soon learn that living in a man's world was not without its difficulties. Bluma, being a true feminist with a spitfire personality, managed to school many doctors who assailed her with unwanted advances. She had no problem standing up to any bully, male or female. The direction of her love life took a few interesting turns in those early days, eventually ending in marriage to a thorny man whom she loved deeply.

In her long life, Bluma managed to be a successful nurse, an entrepreneur who ran her own nursing home, a wife, a mom of two successful children, a painter, and a writer, among many other accomplishments. Explaining the reasons for her memoir, she writes, "I have revived my story for myself with joyful recognition and with a deeper understanding of the past. I present my life now in the hope that my remembrances will be to others a source of history and a guide to creative living" (260–61).

Bluma passed at the age of 109, leaving us with her memories; "As I approach the threshold of completeness, time becomes universal. I am all ages simultaneously" (19). This memoir is proof that regardless of what you are born into, how you spend your life is not predetermined and is completely up to you.

Danielle Palumbo

Interview with President Joe

"What should I wear?" I ask Kinsella. "Probably that," he replies, motioning to the school casual that I'm wearing. So, as I walk down the hallway toward the President's office, dressed in my very best "probably that," you would have thought it was a movie set.

The hallway is deceptively long. The walls are brown, classical and warm, yet opaque. They seem too narrow as I approach the glass door, until it swiftly opens away from me, the pleasant woman behind the counter pushing a button to allow entrance.

"How can I help you?"

I tell her meekly that I am here to interview President Joe. Ten minutes late and evidently underprepared, I fear that I have already made a bad impression. What happened to the version of me who thought, "I am going to interview President Joe!" determined and confident, when presented with the list of interviewees from which his name was absent?

Surreal space lingers as I am led to his office, just through another entryway, and his secretary Kathryn Mason brings him a mug of freshly-made coffee. The air is suddenly constrained, serious. The Osprey President is not wearing "probably that," the semi-expected khaki shorts and Hawaiian shirt. Be not afraid; he smiles.

"It's good to see you," he says, and he motions for me to have a seat. As it turns out, he would have been my mirror in apparel-mood, if not for having to film in the lower level Special Collections area that day.

The next thirty-some minutes of conversation were spent melting severity away. I am grateful to be able to say that President Joe is just as he presents himself. He is strongly casual, open, and intelligent: truly a supporter of student interest.

Some time ago, in the class when details of this interview were arranged, one of my peers proposed the theory that if you stand in the middle of the campus center, clap three times, whistle a tune and spin in a circle, President Joe will certainly appear.

I understand she was merely joking, but my experience heading into President Joe's office, as well as what follows – his input about the library – leads me to believe she may be onto something.

Shannon. How do you define the current library?
President Joe. I think it is antiquated. While staff work to provide modern service, the library isn't conducive to this. It's like trying to put a square peg in a round hole. There are limitations. But, in general, in the past I think libraries were research centers. Now, they are more a center of academic activity, which we have and that's great.

Q. Is there anything you will miss about the library after renovations? (Assuming you are keeping what means the most to you!)
A. I'm not sure. The Holocaust Resource Center means a lot to me. Hopefully the thing I do like the most about the current library will only keep growing – the community.

Q. What do you think is the most important aspect of the library?
A. Physically, I think being a user-friendly space with opportunities is important. From a programmatic standpoint, those opportunities are all built on gathering. The kind of gathering by students we see shows us how it is being used and what the community wants the library to be.

Q. Any pieces the library offers which you would recommend?
A. I always recommend looking at the historical displays. They offer so much to learn. As far as any specific special collection, I don't really have anything outstanding coming to mind there. But, from collections and all around Stockton, I think artwork is also highly significant. Students and staff shouldn't miss it. One of my goals personally is for there to be more artwork in the new library, and all around campus."

Q. I have been told that you actually grew up around Stockton, and that your mother attended. Is this true? Did you interact with the library as a child? How?
A. My mother was a non-traditional student while she was here. I was middle-school aged at the time, so I wasn't too young but also not old enough to really have interacted too much. And, to be honest, there wasn't a whole lot here back then. A lot has changed.

Q. What do you see as different or the same in the current library? What do you think of these changes? (From the past to now).
A. In the past, I think libraries have had a narrow relationship to surrounding communities. They were very separate from the community. Now, over the last decade or so, they have become much more integrated into everyday life, in ways that were previously thought impossible. For example, we have coffee shops in libraries now. That was unimaginable decades ago, and says a lot about the kinds of spaces libraries are becoming.

Q. What is your experience reconceptualizing libraries?
A. As Vice President, I had a great focus on building a learning commons. At other institutions, I have used libraries as a guide for our library here; for instance, up in Connecticut, the library when I started there was brand new. I have also visited other libraries nationally and internationally and gotten great impressions.

Q. What do you think will change – or in this case, what do you plan to change – once the library begins renovations? Any reasoning behind this?
A. It is actually not so much about me at all. The decisions being made are from the community. It is completely community-led. I have seen some of the early plans and blueprints for renovations, and those reflect good research. There is a strong correlation between what I have seen, and what our community is planning. I think the biggest change will be what we already see happening, the renovated library becoming a communal space.

Q. I recognize that students are your number one interest here at Stockton. Ideally, how do you see students using the future library?
A. I want students to be proud of their library. I want it to be a destination for students of comfort, safety, and community where they can not just find tools but immerse themselves in those tools. I would also love to connect to more of our surrounding community here in Atlantic County. We are a public institution, after all; when they see our renovated library or even the one we have now, I hope that they will feel invited and want to join in on the use of our space.

Interviewed by Shannon McGivney

The Stories Untold

Housed on the lower level of the Stockton University library, beyond the haunted stairwell (or elevator – it is sometimes difficult to tell), tucked into a brightly lit corner, you will find Special Collections and Archives. The Bjork Library is open to all students, but many don't know that they have access to these collections. Many aspects of the history of South Jersey are preserved here: stories of individuals, towns, structures, or events. The stories are told through books, maps, photographs, letters, digital materials, and more. Deeply rooted in the idea of such collections is an appreciation for all artifacts that can tell a story, or part of one. Seemingly inconsequential materials may be the vehicles through which important history is passed down to us, and it is through these items that students, community members, and scholars find historical meaning.

My entire life, I have lived along the dividing line of the long enduring rivals of Weymouth and Estell Manor (on the Weymouth side). My youthful knowledge of the local history derived only from the folklore told by grandparents and friends, diluted by word of mouth over the years. I heard rumblings of a disgruntled wife of the mayor who had taken a pencil to the town map and redrawn its borders, cutting anyone she did not like out of the boundaries of Estell Manor. The tale was used to explain why the town borders were so misshapen and why half of people's backyards were in one town and half in the other. The story that had been passed down was of a mean spirited, petty wife.

What I found in the Estell collection in Special Collections is a very different tale. Rebecca Estell Bourgeois did in fact take a red pencil to the town borders, but she was not some irritable wife of a mayor: she was the mayor herself, the first mayor of Estell Manor and the first female mayor in New Jersey. Rebecca Estell Bourgeois had drawn all members of the Democratic party into Estell Manor and all other parties onto the Weymouth side. The story I had been told most of my life was now proved false, and my faith in feminism has been restored – all due to one simple trip past a few ghosts down to the lower level of the library (don't say basement).

Brooke Armitage

The 2024 Literature Seniors, alongside Tom Kinsella in Special Collections and Archives, finding that comfort, safety, and community that President Joe was hoping for.

Left Behind

Extras we don't want to lose.

An Afternoon in the Library Learning Commons

As she had done many times before, Kate entered Stockton's library in search of her roommates, ready to catch up about their day. Many familiar faces sit in the learning commons on the main level, waving to Kate as she scans the room. Dozens of students are gathered around tables, booths, and computer desks, some working diligently and others gossiping freely.

From across the room in the last booth, Kate hears someone call her name. Her ears perk up and she sees Kayla, her roommate. A smile spreads across her face as she sees each of her roommates gesturing to her to come sit with them.

"Where have you been?" Danielle asks. "We've been waiting for you for twenty minutes!"

"Sorry, guys. I stayed back at the end of class to talk to my professor," Kate explains. She takes a seat next to Danielle, inching herself into the booth.

Kate notices both of her friends have their laptops open, ready to work, though Danielle's screen is blank. This was typical library behavior for them.

"I have two hours until my next class so I really need to get started on my paper. It's due this weekend," Kate says. She unzips her backpack to reveal a sea of papers and projects, all loosely thrown inside. Sifting through, she finds her laptop and pulls it out to begin work.

Five minutes of silence go by, broken by a question from Kayla.

"So, how was class today for you guys?"

"Pretty good," Danielle answers, choosing not to elaborate.

"Long and tiring," Kate says, thinking about the almost two-hour lectures she had to sit through today. "I hate having two classes back to back. I can barely stay awake!"

As the conversation continues between the three girls, the screens on their laptops slowly dim and then turn off completely. Danielle talks about the coffee she bought this morning, describing it as the "best coffee she's ever had," followed by Kate and Kayla sharing their opinions about last night's episode of their favorite TV show.

Checking her phone after what she thought was twenty minutes, Kate sees that she only has ten minutes before her next class.

"Guys, it's already 2:20! I have to leave for class!"

Glances are exchanged between the three before laughter erupts from the table. Another day spent in the library, chatting and enjoying time with each other rather than doing homework. Naively, they thought that today would be the day they finally got to work in the library. Not today.

Kate DeFouw

The Descent Into Darkness

Think of a haunted location. The typical places that come to mind include houses, prisons, hospitals, even hotels. Most wouldn't consider a college, especially a newer college, to be haunted; however, any place can be home to a ghost.

Built in the 1970s, Stockton University is a fairly young and modern school. Not a place to suspect pesky spirits. I know that when I first enrolled I did not sense anything out of the ordinary: no sixth sense feelings of an invisible someone occupying a room or unexplained temperature shifts – none of those stereotypical supernatural occurrences that Hollywood popularizes. Not until the spring semester of my freshman year did I notice anything out of the ordinary.

Like many freshmen living on campus, I was finding the adjustment to college life difficult, even well into my second semester. I was struggling to make friends and my academic anxiety was worse than ever since I was focused on maintaining my 4.0 gpa. Since the beginning of school in September, I was usually in the library until closing time, 10 pm. I was there so often that the librarians knew me by name and were surprised whenever I wasn't one of the last people to leave the library.

I love the library at Stockton, especially at night when most other students have called it quits on study sessions or last-minute projects. It was a safe-haven for me, providing me with a place to work outside of my dorm room, which I did not find conducive to studying. Nothing against my roommate at the time; she was lovely. I just wanted my own space. My favorite place to work was the second-floor quiet zone located near huge windows where one could look out toward the woods and Lake Fred. Not many students frequented this area. I did not find the library creepy at night; rather, I found it peaceful. Rarely were others at the library until closing, so more often than not I had the second floor to myself.

Nothing felt off or spooky while I studied alone sitting by the upper level stacks. The only thing that scared me – and it scared me silly – was the closing announcement made by librarians over the PA system. That announcement, even though I knew it was coming, broke the silence out of nowhere and took me by surprise almost every night.

Typically, ten to fifteen minutes before closing a librarian would walk the entire library counting the number of students still working and noting their whereabouts. They didn't want to lock anyone inside at night, so they would warn the students that the library was closing shortly. It was on one of these occasions that my perception of the library changed.

It was the middle of February and I was working on an essay for one of my General Studies classes. It was that time of the night when the librarians warned students of the imminent closing. At this point, being the socially anxious introvert that I was (and still am), I did not interact much with the librarians. We would offer each other a pleasant smile and the occasional "hello," but nothing beyond that. I was alone on the upper level when the librarian approached me.

"Hi," the middle-aged lady said as she stood by my desk, "I just wanted to let you know that we will be closing in about ten minutes."

"Okay, thank you for letting me know," I responded, starting to wrap up the charger for my laptop. I thought that was the end of our interaction. That was how it usually went. But tonight was different because the librarian didn't walk off.

"I don't know how you stay up here by yourself every night," she said while looking around the deserted library.

"Excuse me?" I didn't know what she was talking about. In my mind, being surrounded by books during the peaceful nighttime with no one else nearby was a great enjoyment. I mean, who doesn't want to be surrounded by books?

"Did no one ever tell you about the ghost?" she asked skeptically, as if she couldn't believe someone would not have heard about the ghost.

"What ghost?" I replied.

Now, let me declare that I *do* very much believe in ghosts. I have always believed in and been fascinated by the supernatural – my whole family believes. So the librarian's comment instantly intrigued me.

She shuffled back and forth a bit. "Well, it's known around here that the library is haunted. People hear voices and see shadows when nobody is around. We have even named the ghost, Frances (or Francis)."

This surprised me since I'd never seen or heard anything odd, but I am easily engrossed by my work and regularly use Airpods while working. It is difficult for me to be distracted by things around me.

"Hmmm, I've never seen anything," I commented, trying not to let my disappointment show.

"Well, most of the encounters come from the back stairwell or the elevator. Anyways, I just wanted to let you know it's almost time to close. I'll see you downstairs in a little bit." And with that – having dumped surprisingly major information on me as though it was nothing – she left.

Up until that night, I had never used the elevator or the back stairwell, but now my curiosity got the best of me. Who was I to turn away the chance to see a ghost? I quickly packed the rest of my belongings and made a point of not putting my earbuds in. I would be fully aware of my surroundings.

I had only a vague idea of where this so-called haunted stairwell was located, so it took me a few minutes to find it. I won't lie, just the hallway leading to it felt off. It had a wall on one side and endless shelves on the other. It felt like I was walking down a tunnel. Shifting my tote bag onto my other shoulder, I pushed open the metal door leading into the stairwell.

Immediately, I knew this felt different. Where the main stairway was bright, walls covered with artwork, this one had blank, yellowish walls and fluorescent lighting. Even the echoes in the stairwell were spooky – and the temperature dropped dramatically. Something was telling me to leave, but I am not a quitter, so I moved down the steps at a regular pace, not wanting to appear afraid.

Whispered noises seemed to accompany the sound of my footsteps. As I moved further down the stairs, I sensed that I wasn't alone. Was something right behind me, stepping as I stepped, but milliseconds after me?

Midway down the staircase, I stopped and took a few breaths to calm my rapid heartbeat . . . this wasn't a good idea. As I stood there, a frigid breeze blew past me, freezing me on the spot. This sudden wind couldn't have been a draft from an open door. The doors at each landing were solid metal fire doors, meaning I would have heard someone opening one. I didn't. The chill swept through me, as if someone were running down the steps in order to beat me to the bottom.

As I stood in fear, I could have sworn I heard faint laughter echoing in the stairwell. Was that a little girl? At this point I couldn't tell whether the laughter was real or my mind playing tricks. I wanted to move, to run out into the library, but it felt as though someone was holding my feet in place.

"Please, please just let me go," I spoke to myself, knowing very well that sobs were about to break through if I had to stay there longer. As if on cue, my body jerked forward, and whatever was holding me finally let go. I wasn't going to waste any more time trying to figure out the logic behind that . . . if there was any logic to this at all. I quickly made my way down the stairs.

And just when it couldn't get any creepier, once I got to the bottom landing, there sat an old-fashioned teacher's desk stored in the dark corner. It reminded me of a desk one would see at the front of a high school classroom, which was strange as I had never seen another like it at Stockton.

I didn't waste time pondering over the desk. I quickly shoved the door open and left the stairwell. Immediately, everything once again felt right with the world. I was free from the liminal space of the stairwell. Just then the PA system boomed, announcing the final warning to leave the library. I won't lie, I jumped, but in my defense I had just gone through significant mental turmoil. I quickly made my way to the front door, throwing a smile and a "goodnight" over my shoulder for the librarians.

After that night, I continued to frequent the library, but something was different. Although I never again used that stairwell, I always felt like I wasn't alone in a room, even when I knew that I was. It always felt as though someone was staring at me from behind the stacks. Honestly, I became a bit paranoid. The realistic, logical side of me knows that no one was there and that it was all in my head, but the side of me that is fascinated by the supernatural truly believes that something followed me from that stairwell.

I'll never know for certain whether the Stockton library is haunted – I will graduate soon and my memories of Stockton will fade – but I will forever be touched by what occurred in that stairwell on that February night. And I may think about it as I sit teaching at my own high school desk.

Gianna Trematerra

Whispered noises seemed to accompany the sound of my footsteps.

Special Collections and Archives:
The Work of Many Hands

How does a new college, opened to the public in 1971, undertake to preserve its ongoing history and that of the much older local community? How did our currently well-organized Special Collections and Archives, significant repositories of local history, get underway?[1] This brief history traces the development of Stockton's Special Collections and Archives from their earliest efforts to the first major donations of South Jersey materials nearly forty years later.[2]

The Stockton Archives

The need for a college archive was recognized early on. A month before classes opened at the Mayflower Hotel in Atlantic City, on August 4, 1971, Herman Elstein, Assistant Director of Reader Services, suggested retention of important school-related documents including academic working papers, trustee meetings, budgets, relevant laws, constructions reports, etc. Arthur Flandreau, Director of the Library, and Richard P. Chaite, assistant to President Bjork, advised that the archives be housed in the "Reader Services" area of the library. At some future date a "Special Collections and Archives" department was to be formed.[3] The archives collection, therefore, began shortly after the college opened as the "College Information File," a miscellaneous collection of college newspapers, college working papers, and information about Richard Stockton, the signer of the Declaration of Independence.[4]

Early planning for the Archives, dating from 1974–1975, recognized similarities in format and handling requirements between archival materials and government documents. It was decided to place the Archives under the supervision of the Government Documents librarian.[5] From

---

1 Stockton faculty and staff who provided details for this history include Lydia Javins, Bill Bearden, David Pinto, Dick Colby, Louise Tillstrom, Cheryl Olson, Mark Demitroff, John Sinton, Tom Ayers, Charla Comer, Alan Delozier, David Roessel, Ken Tompkins, Heather Perez and Tom Kinsella.
2 A more detailed report on the history of Stockton's Special Collections and Archives, dated July 29, 2022, is preserved in Special Collections and Archives. This essay is a condensed version of that report.
3 Alan Delozier, *The Richard Stockton College of New Jersey Archival Field Guide & Catalog, 1969–1994*, 7.
4 Ginny Vail, "Archives Position Paper," 1982, 1.
5 [McDonald, Joseph], "Stockton Archive Collection Draft," [1974?].

early on, the Archives were considered something of a "step-child."⁶ Government Documents initially resided in the Documents Workroom, E-222, a quite small space. By 1977, it had been relocated to E-004, a twenty by ten foot storage room in the lower level of the library. After the library expansion in 1995, Government Documents grew to encompass a considerable area with multiple rooms in the northeastern corner of the lower level of the library.

The scope of the Archives was deliberately limited. "The college archives collection is to be a select collection of the central documents relating to the development of the institution. It is not intended to be a comprehensive collection detailing all of the activities at the college or is it meant to be a warehouse of files from the various college offices."⁷ The plan developed in 1974–1975 and adopted shortly thereafter was for the archives to be subsumed under the direction of the Government Documents department and to become the responsibility of the Public Services/Documents librarian."⁸

In 1975, non-current materials from the President's office were added to the "College Information File." This may have been when early documents, charred but not destroyed during the arson of the President's cabin (February 1973), were deposited within the archives. For years afterward, the scent of charred paper was evident when certain file cabinets were opened. During fall 1975, approval was granted to Ken Stow, Assistant to the Vice President for Business and Finance, to gather and preserve in the archives annual budget proposals, yearly program guides, development documents, proposals, consultant reports and newspaper articles/promotional publications.⁹ In July 1976, Elizabeth Alton donated copies of her manuscript *The Stockton Story, A History of the Founding of Richard Stockton State College* along with a collection of letters, notes, press clippings, and other documents from the early to mid 1960s that recorded efforts to found the institution.

Initially, the space reserved for the College Archives was a four-drawer vertical file cabinet located in the public area outside of the Documents Workroom (E-222). The collection was closed, with no browsing allowed unless prearranged with the Documents Librarian or Assistant Director for Public Services. By July 1977, the Stockton Archives consisted of three file cabinets and three shelves of records.¹⁰

6 Ginny Vail, "Archives Position Paper," 1982, 1.
7 Wilson M. Stahl, "Discussion Paper on College Archives," July 8, 1981, 1.
8 "Stockton Archive Collection Draft," 1974, 1; Ginny Vail, "Archives Position Paper," 1982, 1.
9 Alan Delozier, *The Richard Stockton College of New Jersey Archival Field Guide & Catalog, 1969–1994*, 8.
10 Alan Delozier, *The Richard Stockton College of New Jersey Archival Field Guide & Catalog, 1969–1994*, 9.

This initial drive to collect materials and to develop the Archives appears to have run out of gas by the late 1970s. In 1981, Reference Librarian Wilson (Bil) Stahl points out the lack of attention accorded to the archives.[11] Ginny Vail, in her 1982 position paper, is scathing:

> Many events have contributed to the total chaos which now exists in archives. First, the estimate of the number of materials to be received was much lower than what has actually been received even though many offices have sent nothing. Second, the constant changes in the college's organization and the even more constant changes in personnel have led to uneven contributions to the archives with many important documents never having been sent at all. In addition, with offices constantly moving and changing names, only an expert with a series of detailed organizational plans could determine where to code each document. Finally, little or no staff has ever been assigned to archives and even then the staff has usually been temporary with little supervision and vague guidelines. In the Documents/Archives department documents has always been considered more important so that even within its own department, archives has been an unwanted step-child, always relegated to "when we have time."[12]

Contributions to the Archives were uneven during the 1980s. "Moribund" may be too strong a word for the collection; perhaps "haphazard" and "understaffed" are better descriptors. With the expansion of the library (funds were earmarked in 1991; construction was completed in 1995) the archives received renewed attention. In February of 1994, Luis Rodriguez, Assistant Director for Public Services, approved student Alan Delozier's independent study within the Stockton Archives. Delozier, who had a degree from St. Bonaventure and was taking additional history courses at Stockton, undertook to organize and refocus the archives; Professor William J. Gilmore-Lehn and Government Documents librarian Frank Wagner supervised his work. Delozier, who would become University Archivist at Seton Hall University, completed an extensive review of the Archives and served as part-time Stockton College Archivist through 1994.

---

11 Wilson M. Stahl, "Discussion Paper on College Archives," July 8, 1981.
12 Ginny Vail, "Archives Position Paper," 1982, 1.

The Beginnings of Special Collections

In February of 1974, Bil Stahl put forward a proposal for the creation of a Pine Barrens Information Center at Stockton.[13] Recognizing the ecological and cultural importance of the Pine Barrens (the Pinelands National Reserve would be established in 1978), Stahl proposed a center that would attract and support scholars and community members studying the Pine Barrens. He envisioned a clearing house with the potential to promote off-campus partnerships. Stahl listed two initial goals: (1) compilation of a bibliography of literature on the Pine Barrens and (2) establishment of an outstanding collection of primary and secondary source materials. Stahl had begun the project in October 1973, assisted by Stockton student John Wessler.

There was considerable interest in the Pine Barrens at this time. John Sinton, Professor of Environmental Studies, organized three well-received conferences focused on the Pine Barrens (1978, 1979, 1980), which garnered considerable interest on campus and within the wider community. Stockton students studied the environment and culture of the Pine Barrens in many courses. Stahl was requesting support for a project that moved well beyond the scope and capability of the library, with the potential to grow into a regional initiative. His application for office space, one staff member (a clerk typist), and modest funding was not supported. What *did* come about was a collection of materials stored in eight file cabinets, now referred to as the Pine Barrens vertical file. The collection preserves a typed bibliography of Pinelands literature/research, dating through the late 1980s, and copies of several hundred articles, pamphlets, booklets, and a lesser number of full-length studies relating to the Pine Barrens.

In spring 1978,[14] Tom Ayers, Instructor in Folklore, taught a course entitled *Folklore and Folklife of New Jersey*. Ayers encouraged students to study folkways of the indigenous Piney culture and

---

[13] Wilson M. Stahl, "A Preliminary Proposal for the Establishment of a Pine Barrens Information Center," February 12, 1974. Pp. 9.

[14] See the article "Naturalist to Speak," for mention of Tom Ayers as Instructor of Folklore and teacher for "Folklore and Folklife of New Jersey," *Stockton Chronicle*, March 13, 1978, 3. Ayers transferred from Concordia College to Stockton in September 1972. He enrolled in a folklore course taught by Mary Ruth Warner, Instructor in Social Sciences. The course inspired both Ayers and Andy Pepper to form the Stockton Folklore Society and led to the Lake Fred Folk Festival (held in A-wing). When Ayers returned from graduate school, John Sinton, Professor of Environmental Studies, encouraged his involvement in Pinelands preservation projects and related topics. Sinton also urged Ayers to teach "Folklore and Folklife of New Jersey," which he did. He taught the same course at Douglas College.

South Jersey culture. Students interviewed longtime community members and submitted reports of their findings, including supporting materials such as audiotapes, drawings, photographs and maps. The reports were preserved within the library. Topics included details of the life of Clifton Maddox, salt hay farming, decoy carving, military folktales, New Jersey garvey building, prohibition and drug lore, women's folklore, construction of a Barnegat Bay sneakbox, and more. While not all projects held great significance, some did. For example, Mark J. Fletcher, for his project, interviewed his neighbor John J. Lingelbach, a pig farmer who had owned a portion of the land that Stockton is built upon. The Fletcher report includes photographs of Lingelbach, Lake Fred, and various outflow conduits, along with a hand-drawn map of the properties purchased by the State of New Jersey in 1969 and 1970. It also includes a cassette tape preserving a seventeen-minute interview with Mr. Lingelbach who describes Lake Fred's history as a cranberry bog. This and other projects completed for Ayers are preserved in Special Collections. Lydia Javins has described them as the protoplasm for what we now refer to as Special Collections.

In fall 1982, a proposal was advanced by Bill Gilmore to establish a South Jersey Archives to be housed within the library. Gilmore pointed out the weak holdings of South Jersey primary sources in the State's largest historical repositories, naming the New Jersey State Archives, the State Library, the New Jersey Historical Society, Rutgers and Princeton. He also noted the fragmented state of holdings by South Jersey historical societies. In contrast to Bil Stahl's earlier Pine Barrens Information Center, Gilmore hoped to focus on the six lower counties of South Jersey (he does not mention Burlington or Ocean counties). He envisioned an archive that would promote engagement with local history among students and academics. The archive did not materialize, presumably lacking institutional support.[15]

In 1988, Ann Corbett was hired to work in the Reference area. With an interest in local history, she began to identify Stockton materials and collections that dealt with South Jersey. She gathered together the student projects from *Folklore and Folklife of New Jersey*, including an earlier photographic essay "Costumes at Stockton," dating from fall 1975, which documents dressing patterns within the Stockton community (see selections from this project starting on page 171). She collected these materials, the Pine Barren's vertical file begun by Bil Stahl, Stockton's complete

---

15 See [William J. Gilmore-Lehn], "Proposal for the Establishment of a South Jersey Archives at Stockton State College," [1982], Pp. 6. Mentioned in Alan Delozier, *The Richard Stockton College of New Jersey Archival Field Guide & Catalog, 1969–1994*, 10.

run of the Pinelands Commission Minutes (1979–), and Pine Barrens focused books, some quite fragile, that had arrived as donations. Cheryl Olson, a student worker in Reference between 1988 and 1990, assisted Corbett in assembling the South Jersey collection and remembers that it was housed in a glass-front room on the main level of the library. Only Corbett and the Circulation Desk had a key to that room.

Not all books in the collection had to do with the Pinelands. Bill Bearden described the selection of titles as haphazard: some books *were* about the Pinelands, some about broader aspects of New Jersey, some were simply older imprints with fragile bindings. These books were housed in two sets of glass-door cabinets, painted white, in the glass-front room, formerly a small individual study room. The locked cabinets were repurposed display cases for minerals donated by Stockton's Division of Natural Sciences and Mathematics. In 1991, Ann Corbett left Stockton. While her efforts had provided early steps toward an organized Special Collections focused on local history and culture, the resulting materials were not immediately deemed important.

In 1995, when the library was renovated and expanded, the Special Collections books were transferred from the small individual study room, which had been demolished during renovations, to a newly built room opposite the Circulation Desk (E-105), larger than the previous space, but not by much. Identified as "The Special Collections Room," the door was kept locked, and Circulation still controlled the key. It was rarely used.

By 1996, when Lydia Javins was hired to work in Circulation, Special Collections had become an orphaned collection. She took an immediate interest and began reviewing and further organizing the collection. Librarian Barbara Ruth Campbell also took an interest, writing a one-page annual report for Special Collections for the year 1997–1998. She estimated that 272 titles were stored in the glass-door cases and expressed an interest in promoting the existence of Special Collections to area school teachers, genealogical societies, historical societies and Pine Barrens groups. Her plans for outreach were laudable, but it is not clear that significant action was completed.

The Development of Special Collections and Archives

In July 2001, David Pinto became Director of the Library and brought to Stockton his interest in special collections. Gerry O'Sullivan, the previous director, had shown no interest in this area. With the assistance of Bill Bearden and Lydia Javins, Pinto began to rethink and reorganize both Special Collections and the Stockton Archives. By 2003, President Farris – who announced her retirement in February 2002, effective at the end of June 2003 – had begun to send box after box of files from her office to the Archives, still situated within the Government Documents area on the lower level. This compounded existing organizational and space problems. It became clear that the badly cluttered Government Documents Workroom (E-056) and the adjacent glass-walled room facing Lake Fred and D-wing (E-056b) had to be reorganized.

Lydia Javins began work in Government Documents in 2005, and upon the retirement of Frank Wagner, the Government Documents librarian, she took over management in September 2006. The unit was to be reimagined as the College Archives, Special Collections, and Government Documents (with the latter deemphasized). In 2006, Javins had the materials stored in the Special Collections room (E-105) opposite Circulation, brought down to the Government Documents area. The cabinets for the Pine Barrens vertical file were moved at some earlier date.

The workroom was a hodgepodge of piles of paper. David Pinto reported that the adjacent glass-walled room, slated to become the "Reading Room" if it could be decluttered, looked like the stateroom scene from the Marx Brothers' *A Night at the Opera!* Furniture was stacked to the ceiling. File cabinets were stacked one atop another, tables on tables, desks on desks. Locks were broken on many file cabinets; keys were missing for others. Various boxes were filled with junk cardboard, and stacks of miscellaneous papers filled the room. Painstakingly, the space was cleared. Special mention goes to Ron Fieros from Circulation for removing the dangerously stacked upper tier file cabinets and hauling them elsewhere and to Wayne Bagnell, from the Key Shop in Plant Management, who spent hours picking and replacing file cabinet locks so that Javins could get key control over the area.

Javins was joined in fall 2005 by Dick Colby, recently retired Professor Emeritus of Cell-Biology. Unpaid, Dick assumed the position of Volunteer College Archivist. He first located and organized for binding the minutes of the Board of Trustees. He then moved on to Middle States accreditation reports. He also organized materials from the Stockton Foundation and the Faculty Assembly, especially focusing on the Library Committee, which he had chaired for many years. Dick straightened out the map collection.

By October 2005, a draft policy for the "Richard Stockton College of New Jersey Archives and Special Collections" was in circulation and, working together, Dick Colby and Lydia Javins brought order out of chaos. They were assisted by students from the Atlantic County Special Services School as paid TES staff, who did an amazing amount of the clerical grunt work necessary to thoroughly reorganize. By 2007, the Archives were evolving into an entity of its own, no longer a step-child. Perhaps for the first time, one could distinguish among Special Collections, the Archives, and Government Documents, with Special Collections and Archives taking the lead as the importance of paper-based Government Documents waned in the digital age. Javins remembers that in 2008, Director David Pinto came downstairs, inspected the department and declared, "We have an Archive!"

Collections Arrive

Starting in September 2006, when Javins took over, the Archives were processed and cataloged as quickly as possible. Whatever the library could afford to bind it had bound. Javins also turned her attention to incoming special collections. She organized the John Henry "Pop" Lloyd Committee Records which arrived starting in 2006. In November 2007, William W. Leap, a local historian from Runnemede, agreed to donate his local history collection to Special Collections, 1,300 titles in various formats: monographs, annuals, maps, atlases, newspaper and magazine articles. All pertained to South Jersey. Materials for a focused and significant Special Collections library had arrived.

Tom Kinsella, Professor of Literature, began actively working with Special Collections and Archives in 2009. Four of his students curated the exhibition *Pages from the Pines: Literature of the Pine Barrens & South Jersey* in February 2010. The exhibition showcased books borrowed from local historian David C. Munn and later donated to Stockton. In fall 2010, another group of Kinsella's students introduced the Leap collection to the Stockton community, curating the exhibition entitled *Exploring South Jersey through the William W. Leap Collection* (November 2010 – January 2011).

At this time the library had three exhibition cases – two small paired jewelry display cases and a larger metal-framed case. Kinsella and Professor David Roessel requested funds from ARHU, approved by Dean Robert Gregg, to construct five additional wooden and glass cases. Additional student curated exhibitions became a regular feature of the library.

When Lydia Javins retired in 2009, she was succeeded by Louise Tillstrom. In 2012, David Pinto, having retired as Library Director, returned as part-time, paid archivist and curator of Special Collections, taking over from Dick Colby. In fall 2012, David C. Munn signed a letter of agreement with Stockton announcing his intention to donate his collection of South Jersey materials to Special Collections. At that time he donated approximately 300 volumes of South Jersey poetry and books authored by John McPhee.

Also in 2012, the old NJN studio in lower E-wing (E-035) was allocated to Special Collections. Employees from the Division of Facilities and Operations constructed a connecting doorway and shelving was installed in 2013 allowing the space to serve as the Special Collections stacks. During May 2013 through 2015, Kinsella secured internal funding to support Stockton's growing Special Collections. The award enabled the restoration of the large F. W. Beers *Topographical Map of Atlantic County* (1872) and funded the retrofitting of locked stacks outside of Special Collections and Archives.

With the arrival of the David C. Munn collection in May 2014, Special Collections at Stockton was no longer an afterthought. Munn's 10,000 item donation, focused on South Jersey, was an important academic resource that needed to be curated and shared. Other smaller collections, such as the Buzby Historic Chatsworth General Store collection and the Budd Wilson collection, were being donated as well. David Pinto was providing excellent, part-time service, but the need for a full-time special collections professional to curate and develop these collections was obvious.

Joe Toth, Director of the Library (2012 to 2021), restructured staffing positions and created the position of Special Collections librarian. In 2017, Heather Perez was hired for the position and, with the excellent assistance of Louise Tillstrom, students and other librarians, has built a flourishing department. To date, approximately 115 additional collections, large and small, have joined the Leap and Munn collections. In important ways, the earlier visions of Special Collections as a repository of materials related to the Pine Barrens and South Jersey have been realized. Today the department preserves and makes available books, images (in photograph, slide, glass slide, negative and digital formats), historic ledgers and business records, letters, oral histories, ephemera, maps, and even eighteenth-century vellum deeds. Documents related to each of the eight southernmost counties of New Jersey come under the purview of Special Collections. The department is well placed to explore unique opportunities offered in our digital age for preservation, dissemination, and study of local heritages.

Stockton's path to its current Special Collections and Archives has had false starts and periods of neglect, but over the years library staff and faculty, often assisted by students, have envisioned something well beyond a storage space for old records. Understanding the importance of place – of Stockton, the Pine Barrens, and South Jersey – they have collected, preserved, and made available appropriate historical materials, and continue to do so. Yet Stockton, at heart, is an institution of teaching and learning. The worth of the collection extends beyond its use for traditional archival research. Special Collections and Archives hold the raw materials for academic studies, podcasts, exhibitions, dramatizations, documentaries, social media postings and more – their usefulness is limited only by the creativity of the user. Think of Stockton Special Collections and Archives as an intellectual maker space that provides copious and rich materials to interested students, faculty and community members alike.

Tom Kinsella

Dear Tom,

In reply to your request for stories about Stockton during my time (1987–2018), I'd like to submit the following items.

A contemporary student would not recognize the Stockton library the year I started on the job. Although we had an online circulation system, the library maintained a card catalog, arranged by author, title, and subject entries, in the public area near the circulation desk. Likewise, we had a card shelflist, arranged by library call number, in the Technical Services office. We cataloged our collection using the OCLC online service database, but ordered paper cards at the same time we set our holdings in that database. Usually, the catalog and shelflist cards arrived within ten days. Library staffers were then assigned the task of filing the cards in the appropriate drawers of the card catalog.

Likewise, when items were found to be lost, they needed to have all their corresponding catalog cards removed. All this activity was enormously labor-intensive. By 1990, Stockton along with New Jersey's seven other libraries belonging to the ALN (Academic Library Network), decided to abandon its shared CLSI online circulation system and plan for an integrated online library system, which put an end to the card catalog and the card shelflist. The first entirely online record we cataloged was in April 1992, and it was a book by John C. Evans, entitled *Tea in China: the History of China's National Drink*. As of this writing, it can still be found on shelf. Some time later, the card catalog was emptied of cards and the entire cabinet was moved to Stockton's Central Stores, where it was auctioned off. Someone told me it was purchased for use as a hardware cabinet – for screws, nuts, bolts, etc. All those drawers in it made it useful for that purpose.

In my early years, the crowding in the library was one of the first things you noticed. Periodical issues had to be piled on the floor, because there was no room on the existing shelves. Shelf space for books was nearly exhausted. Paper indexes took up much shelf space. Our first electronic indexes for periodical articles arrived in the early 1990s. The H. W. Wilson indexing company provided these indexes on CD-ROMs. A librarian would insert the CDs into three workstations to allow users access to the indexes. When the library closed for the day, the CDs would be removed and placed in storage. H. W. Wilson designed some fancy looking screen graphics for these new indexes. Some librarians drolly noted: "The flashing lights attract the serious scholars." But they would quickly replace paper indexes more and more, until, within a few years, the indexes were all available via the Internet. What a technological breakthrough!

One of the student study rooms was designated as Stockton's Special Collections Room. The small collection was housed in a former mineral display cabinet which had been donated by the Geology Program. Stockton President Peter M. Mitchell (1979–1983), whose scholarly background was colonial America, donated a number of items to the special collections. These included two Richard Stockton autographs and a 1776 edition of the laws of the province of New Jersey, printed in Burlington. President Mitchell accepted a bust of Richard Stockton, a gift of the Class of 1982, which was displayed in K-Wing for years until it was moved to the library with the 1995 library renovation.

Before the renovation, many of the currently occupied spaces were used for other purposes. The entire space in front of the current Holocaust Resource Center was designated Late Study and was open for student use until 2 am. A part of the library's present Electronic Classroom was used for storage. Since the G-Wing cafeteria was not open in the evening or on weekends, the present Constantelos Reading Room was the library's lounge, which the staff could use for meal breaks.

The library renovation/expansion was an important event, well-remembered by all who participated. By that time, the Holocaust Resource Center was beginning and it was thought a special space was needed to store the Center's survivor interviews on videotape. A bank safe was donated and is still located on the ground floor. Significantly, the safe was installed and the new, expanded space was constructed around it. Former GENS Dean Jan Colijn joked that my job at Stockton was secure since I was the only one who could successfully open the safe.

The pre-expansion library used to end where, on the main level, the doors leading to the exedra area and the elevator are now. Because Stockton was expanding towards Lake Fred on land protected by the Pinelands Commission, it was necessary to get the Commission's permission for the new building. In the one area they refused to give a permit – the area between the service road in the back and D-Wing – it was necessary to leave the area undeveloped to satisfy them. We in the library called it "The Notch" and it is still visible.

I don't know of any ghost in the elevator, but do remember the ghost in the old stairwell near the current elevator. I never heard or saw anything myself, but felt extremely uneasy at being alone there. Anyone who has had the experience would not wish to loiter.

Bill Bearden

Costumes at Stockton

A selection of photographs from a class project preserved in Special Collections and Archives dating from fall 1975.

Richard E. Bjork, first president of Stockton, after whom the library is named. This is the opening photograph in the collection, setting a fashion tone against which other photos contrast.

Dorothy MacEachern

College Chaplain Father Joe Waggenhoffer

Bill Lubenow, Professor of History

Marcia and Joye (last names not provided) in the G-Wing cafeteria.

Jeanne-Andrée Nelson, Professor of French, and student.

Tonia Thompson

Pat Sexton

 Richard (no last name provided)

 Bonnie Bigley

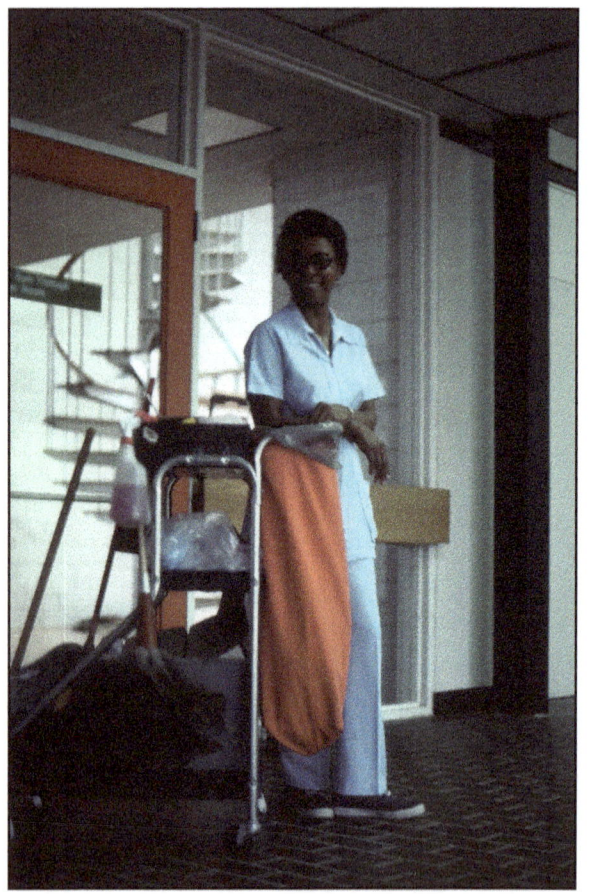 

Lilyan Farrell　　　　　　　　　　Saul Porcellini

Nellie Callan   Stuart Stow

Jan Angelecci Karen Butterhof

Z Group (as captioned)

Doris the Doll (as captioned)

California Surfer (as captioned)

Construction Documents

The following floor plans record the state of the Library Learning Commons project in November 2024. DIGroup Architecture and the Stockton Division of Facilities and Operations developed the design in consultation with the University administration, Library staff, Information Technology Services, and Stockton students, faculty and staff. Thanks in particular to Don Hudson, Skip West, Dan Sernotti, and Marcie Pallante along with Scott Huston and his excellent team.

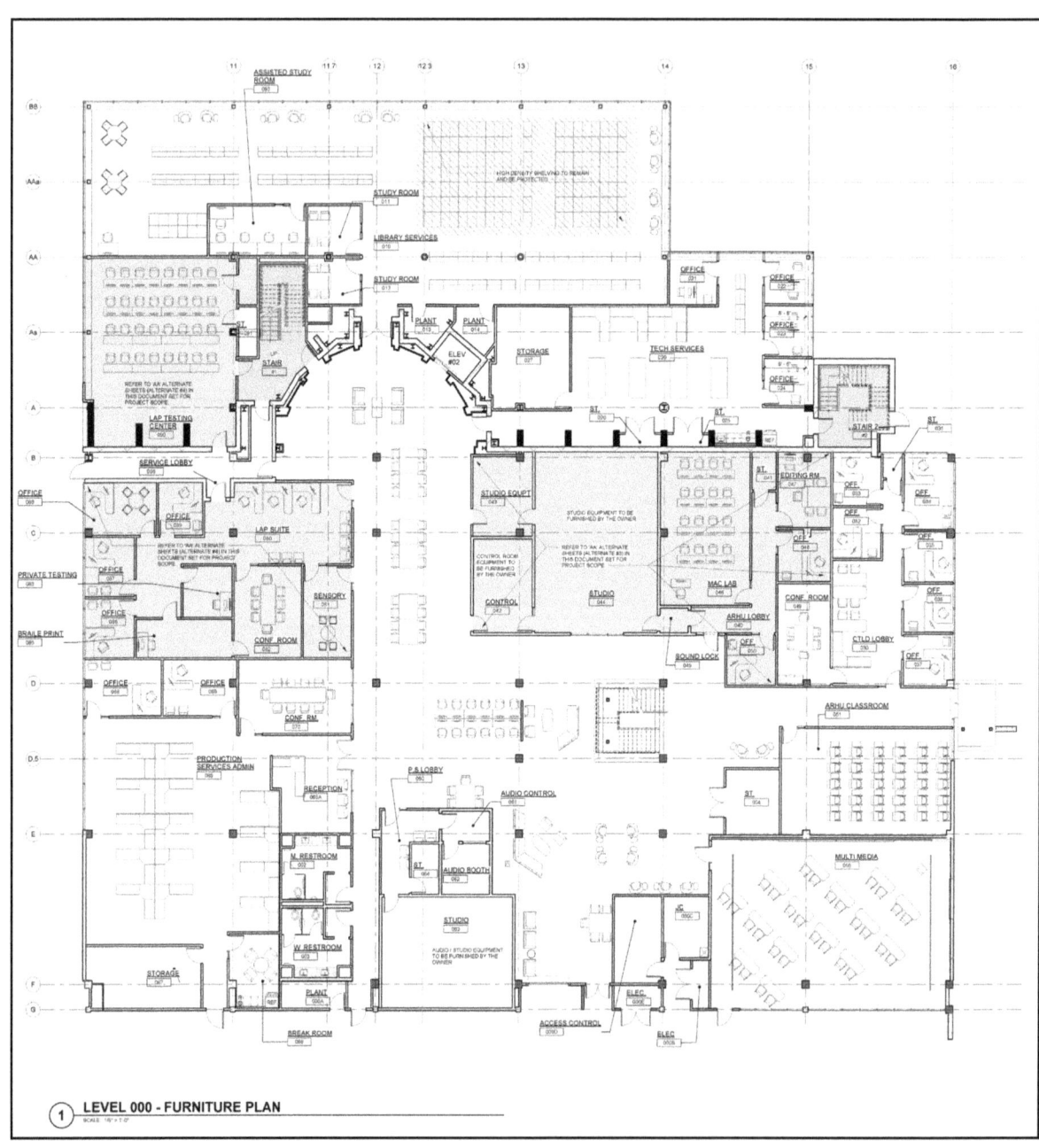

1. LEVEL 000 - FURNITURE PLAN

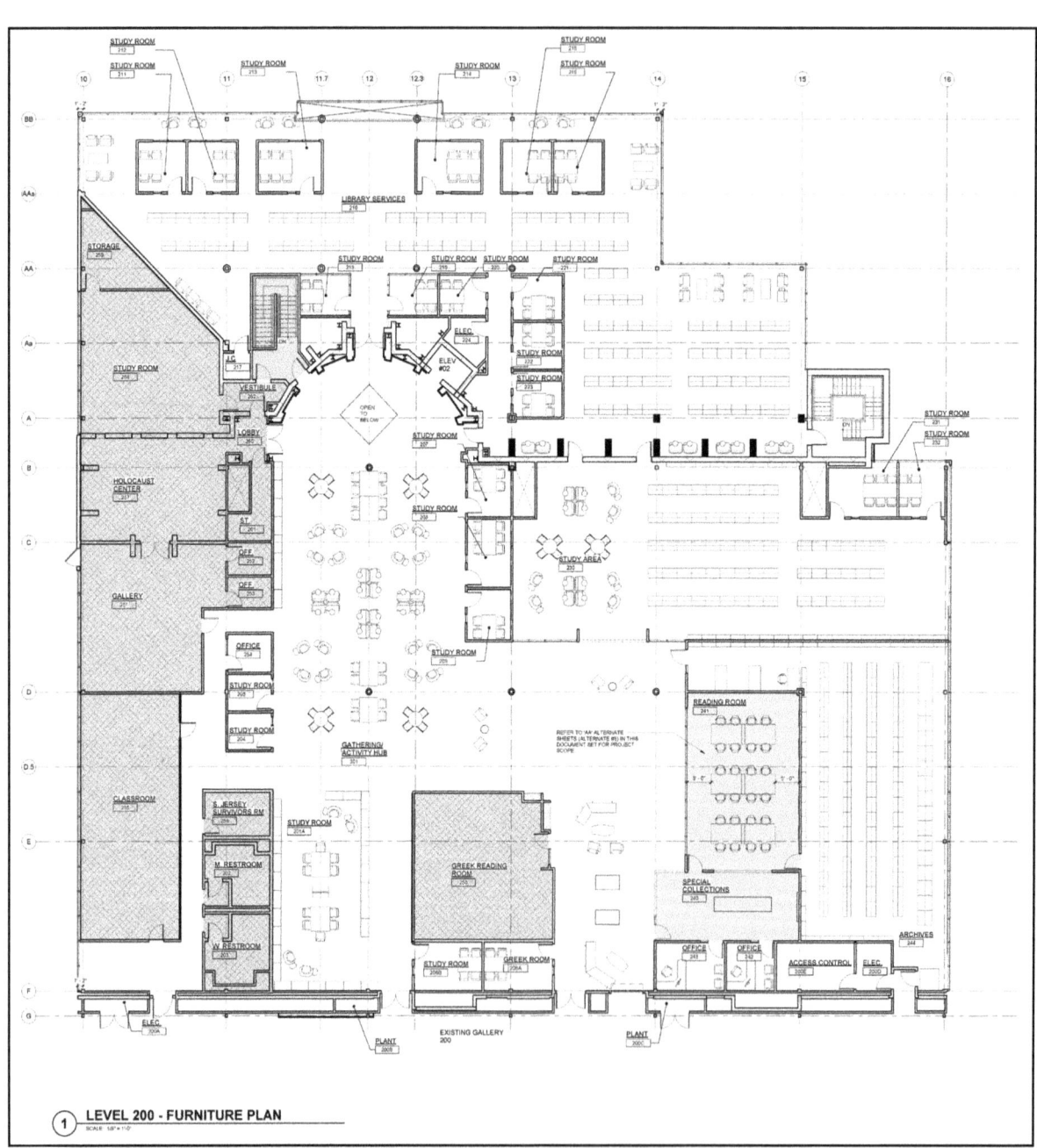

Kindred Spirits

As I made my way from the barren stacks of the Lower Level into Special Collections and Archives, I wasn't sure what I would find. It was a room I had never entered before, a place that I only vaguely knew existed. It didn't feel right for me to be there, walking among these historical documents with my clunky book bag and dirt-covered Doc Martens. I felt like a disturbance as I peeked my head into the back room, asking gently for Heather Perez, as I'd made an appointment on the online calendar (I think?). I had made notes of a few things I wanted to look at, but as soon as Heather asked me what I wanted her to pull out first, I was drawn to the Ephraim Ogden Journal Collection (number U0055, if you're interested, which I think you should be).

The journal itself was old, from 1804, written by Ephraim Ogden, a schoolhouse teacher in a village of Quaker students and parents. It starts with his list of rules for the school, including one that states that students should behave "without the least laughter or unnecessary talk," which led me, as a future teacher, to think okay bud, good luck with that. It was kind of hilarious, reading these old rules and picturing this man forcing students to sit under their desks for 30 minutes as a punishment for "misbehaving." I knew I wouldn't want him as a teacher.

And yet I felt a kinship with him. As I gently flipped through the journal, I found myself intrigued by this long dead man. Could he imagine where his words ended up? Who would end up reading them? By reading them alone, creating this image of him in my head, was he resurrected in a way? Would he have slapped me for whispering to my friend about lesson plans in class earlier?

I don't know the answers to these questions. I know that I thought about them as I continued on my day, and made another appointment down in Special Collections. I wondered. So, I made my way down the next week, ready to read again, curious to see what else I might find.

Then I found the second part of the collection: Bill Leap's research. This took up nearly twice as much space as the journal and its transcription. It was made up of genealogical information about Ephraim Ogden and family, research into the location of the journey he described in his journal, maps, research into where his school was, and relevant photographs. Much of it was handwritten, either in cursive or in shorthand. It had random notes and lattice tables, and at one point a reference to the IRS in the margins. But it was filled with information, about Ogden, sure, but also Leap.

I had never met Bill Leap; before now, I hadn't known he existed. Yet here I was, reading his notes and maps, trying to make sense of what he had written. I wanted to talk to him so badly, to meet another person who had fallen down this rabbit hole of a long dead teacher who played some sort of whale instrument in the woods to prank the Quakers. But all I had were the notes he had left. There was a book draft that had multiple versions of a first chapter on legal pad paper, a printout of an eBay listing for a whale ocarina, dozens of maps, and many, many pages of notes. Some of them were easy to follow, many were not. That was the best part.

Inside these notes and writings were pieces of Bill Leap. Drawings, reminders, perhaps an attempt to file his taxes. Ogden's journal had the same thing – drawings, random numbers, and starting and stopping sentences, like he wasn't sure what he wanted to preserve. It prompted me to go back through my own notes, to see what bits of myself I had left in there. Most of it makes sense, I think, but I particularly enjoy the bullet point that just says "lattice method win." In twenty years, will anyone know what that means? Will anyone know why I decided it was important to write down "star spangled paper" or "silly little girl brain?" Or are these the parts of me that will linger on, baffling future students at Stockton?

Ephraim Ogden's words continued past his death to Bill Leap through his journal. Bill Leap's words continued past his death to me through Special Collections. Even if I'm not dead, my words from this version of myself will hopefully continue to you in this book, dear reader. And who knows what they might inspire?

Sarah Coe

Bill Leap's notes, alongside Sarah Coe's: The Ephraim Ogden Journal collection.

Afterword

Hidden among the pines, a college was built and, hidden along the spine of the college, the library. Hidden "within the stacks" is our past, present, and future, a collision of the real and the imagined. Libraries have long been the living, breathing past documenting what and who and why and where. Many of those involved in this project walked into the library as students and are leaving as scholars. All of us regardless of how or why we came here have, in small and large ways, been influenced and impacted by the books, the people, the organization, and the culture of the library, this library. And you, the reader, are part of the beating heart of the library heard before the first foundation was dug and echoing well into the unforeseeable future.

How do we balance what we've seen of the past with that of the future? Our authors have highlighted the past and present of some of the documents and inhabitants of our library. At this point in history, we look back and study the past and wonder whether or not that past will be repeated in our future. Do we learn from the past or look to the digital future and artificial intelligence? We know that the library is a mixture of both the past and the technology of the future. Libraries and librarians must stay on the breaking edge of these technologies in order to teach the students of the present, allowing us to look into the past and create some sort of meaning out of it all.

In the 2002 film adaptation of H. G. Wells book *The Time Machine*, librarians are replaced by "fusion powered photonic with verbal and visual link capabilities connected to every database on the planet" or rather a graphical human-looking interactive artificial intelligence. While virtual assistants are here to stay, librarians and those who work in libraries still have a place not only to help us when computer prompts cannot get us to the information we need but as guides to repositories of the past as we inch ever closer to the future – the Future that our science fiction often gets right, or at least in "practical application" (Dr. Alexander Hartdegen's character in *The Time Machine*, 2002).

The future of Stockton's library is being reshaped as the renovation progresses. We all have dreams as to what the library could be, and the reality of what it is will be unveiled as the project continues. Libraries have long been a place of solace but also a place of inspiration and creativity. Sometimes the library has faced scathing rebuke and rebellious action, but it continues to be a backbone of the university.

As we finish the last pages of this book, the original location of the library lies vacant, no one to "shhhhh" the inhabitants who have all been relocated during this reimagining. These quiet, hushed spaces paused in the dark are akin to the bedtime story told late at night to those lying awake with breaths held in suspense, waiting for the last page to be turned and the story to be revealed. Our story is here, in this place, these people, and the timelessness of the library.

Christy W. Goodnight

Index

Adventures in Idealism: The Life of Professor H. L. Sabsovich, Founder of Woodbine, New Jersey, Katharine Sabsovich, 53–54
Altagracia, Taina, *83–84*
Alton, Elizabeth B., 37–38, 129–30, 160
Amendolar, Samuel, 4
Angelecci, Jan, 180
Argo, The, 22
Armitage, Brooke, 4, *11*, *117*, *129–30*, *146*
Atlantic Blueberry Company collection, 138
Atlantic City: Its Early and Modern History, Alexander Barrington Irvine, 119–120
Atlanticare's History of Caring, 37
Ayers, Tom, 159, 162

Back to the Land: Alliance Colony to the Ozarks in Four Generations, Ruth Weinstein, 115–16
Bagnell, Wayne, 165
Barbie, Greta Gerwig, 129–30
Barnabei, Nicole, 105–106
Bearden, Bill, 86, 159, 164, *169–70*
Beauty is Never Enough, Elizabeth B. Alton, 129–30
Bertolino, Joe, 15, 143–45, 147
Bigley, Bonnie, 177
Birds, The, 30

Bjork, Richard E., 37, 50, 159, 173
Boardwalk Empire, Nelson Johnson, 99
Brady, Amanda, *105–106*, *115–16*
Break-Up-A-Cold Tablets, 58
Brignola, Jena, 4
Butenhoff, Matt, 29
Butterhof, Karen, 180
Buzby's Chatsworth General Store collection, 58, 167

California Surfer, 182
Callan, Nellie, 179
Campbell, Barbara Ruth, 164
Campus Building, 4
Carnesworth, 119–120
Chaite, Richard P., 159
Chamberlain, George Agnew, 59–60
Clinton, Hillary, 21
Crying Voices and Unheard Sounds, 51–52
Coe, Sarah, *55–56*, *135–36*, *187–90*
Colby, Dick, 159, 165, 166
Colijn, Jan, 170
Comer, Charla, 73–81, 159
Connelly, Maddy, 65
Constantelos, Demetrios, 55, 170
Corbett, Ann, 163, 164
Cox, Lisa E., 33
Cranwell, Laura, 128
Cullick, Hannah, 65

Dalí, Salvador, artwork, 35, 36, 93

Darth Vader, 44, 117
Dean, Anisah, *85–93, 119–120*
Defouw, Katherine, 4, *151–52*
Delozier, Alan, 159, 160, 161, 163
Demitroff, Mark, 159
Demosthenes, Shekhania, 35–36
DeStasio, Joyce, 137–39
Devine, Jack, 10
DIGroup Associates, 183
Disney, Walt, 48
Divergently, 51
Doris the Doll, 182
Dune, Frank Herbert, 63

Early Recollections and Life of Dr. James, 83–84
Educational Opportunity Fund, 44
Elstein, Herman, 159
Ephraim Ogden collection, 187–90
Estell Bourgeois, Rebecca, collection, 146
Everyday Adventures, Samuel Scoville Jr., 25–26

Farmer's Daughter: Bluma, A, Bluma Bayuk Rappoport Purmell, 141–42
Farrell, Lilyan, 178
Farris, Vera King, 164–65
Fazio, Pat, 139
Fieros, Ron, 165
Fletcher, Mark J., 163
Frances (or Francis) the ghost, 154

Garment Workers of South Jersey, Nine Oral Histories, 33–34
Geddes, Brecher, Qualls and Cunningham, 70
Gerwig, Greta, 129–30
Gherardi, Franca Fiori, 33
Gilmore-Lehn, William J., 161, 163
Goodnight, Christy W., 137, 139, 191–92
Gregg, Robert, 166

Hanlon, Sarah, 139
Hartdegen, Alexander, 191
Heracane, 21–24
Holocaust Resource Center, Sara & Sam Schoffer, 150, 170
Hudson, Don, 183
Huston, Scott, 183

Irvine, Alexander Barrington, 119–120

Javins, Lydia M., 85–95, 159, 163, 164, 165, 166
Jeitner, Eric, 109–14, 139
Joye, 175

Kelly, Elizabeth, 23–24
Kidd, Calvin, 13
Kidd, Susan, 13
Kinsella, Tom, 7, 11, 57–58, 73, 75, 80, 86, 93, 112, 143, 147, *159–68*, 166, 167, 169
Koster, Arthur Hollis, 104

Lake Fred, 11, 51, 90, 133, 151, 153, 161, 165, 170
Lake Fred Folk Festival collection, 37, 162, 165, 170
Landis, Charles K., 135–36
Lantern on the Plow, The, George Agnew Chamberlain, 59–60
Lanzoni, Nicole, *17–18, 37–39, 73–81*
Last Good Time, The, Jonathan Van Meter, 99
Leap, William, collection, 89–90, 166, 167, 187–90
Levin, John, 115, 116
Lewis, William J., 71–72
Liberto, Anne, 33–34
Library construction plans, 12 (1972), 66–69 (1995), 183–86 (2024)
Lines on the Pines, 57
Lingelbach, John, 90, 91, 163
Lloyd, John Henry "Pop," Committee Records, 166
Lobiondo, Frank, 102
Lombardo, Jaimelyn, 117, 139
Lubenow, William, 174

MacEachern, Dorothy, 173
Mainland Auxiliary of the Atlantic City Medical Center Records (collection), 37–39
Marcia, 175
Marino, Anthony, 50
Marsico, Emma, *35–36, 103–104*
Martinelli, Patricia, 55–56

Martorano, Jessica, 19, 20, 121, 139
Mayflower Hotel, 12, 159
McDonald, Joseph, 159
McGivney, Shannon, *97–98, 143–45*
McMillan, Grant, 4
McPhee, John, 167
Meet The Robinsons, 48
Microfiche machines, 82
Mitchell, Peter M., 170
Moore, Emma Van Sant, 104
Moss, Miriam S., 40–42, 133
Moss, Sydney, 41
Mr. Pothead, 102
Munn, David, collection, 132, 166–67
Myers, Liz, *21–24*

Nagiewicz, Steve, 50
Nelson, Jeanne-Andrée, 175
Niceler, Marissa, 16
Northside, The, Nelson Johnson, 99
Noyes, Ethel, 90

O'Connor, Luke, 19, 121, *122–27*
Ogden, Ephraim, collection, 187–90
Olson, Cheryl, 87, 93, 159, 164
Orlowski, Victoria, *33–34, 51–52, 137–39*
O'Sullivan, Gerald, 164
Our Stories, Ourselves, 51
Out of Doors Club, The, Samuel Scoville Jr., 107–108
Outfit, The, Charles "Budd" Wilson Jr., 103–104

Pallante, Marcie, 183
Palumbo, Danielle, *99–101*, *141–42*
Pepper, Andy, 162
Perez, Heather, 8, 37, 57–58, 99–101, 128, 132, 137, 139, 159, 167, 187
Performing Arts Center, 30–32
Phillips, Noah, 115–116
Pinelands Folklife Photograph collection, 37
Pinto, David, *7–8*, 85, 88, 90, 159, 164, 165, 166, 167
Plumb and Rose (artwork), 35, 36, 93
Pool (gone but not forgotten), 30–32
Porcellini, Saul, 178
Precious (the cat), 96
Previti, Shilo Virginia, 4
Punktuations, The, 138, 139
Purmell, Bluma Bayuk Rappoport, 141–42

Richard, 177
Riehl, Cheyenne, 27–29
Rodriguez, Luis, 161
Roessel, David, 159, 166
Rose, Robert E., Dr. (collection), 18, 37

Sabsovich, H. L., 53–54
Sabsovich, Katharine, 53–54
Scarduzio, Mary, 34
Scooby Doo, 45
Scoville, Samuel, Jr., 25–26, 107–108
Seasons, Dallas Lore Sharp, 17–18, 97–98
Seasons in the Pine Barrens: The Journal of Miriam S. Moss, 40–42, 133
Seneca Falls Convention, 22
Sernotti, Dan, 183
Sexton, Pat, 176
Sharp, Dallas Lore, 17–18, 97–98
Shockley, Gabrielle, *43–48*, *59–60*
Short Story dispenser, 20
Simpsons, The, 43
Sinton, John, 159, 162
Skywalker, Luke, 44
Slocum, Carol, 16
Special Collections, 128, 147 (work room), 158 (the stacks)
Spirit of '48, 21–24
Stahl, Wilson M., 160, 161 162, 163
Stamatopolous, Gus, 61–64
Still, James, Dr., 83–84
Stockpot Literary Magazine, 22, 51–52
Stockton, Richard, 7, 170
"Stockton is my Home," Lydia M. Javins, 94–95
Stockton Story, A History of the Founding of Richard Stockton State College, The, Elizabeth B. Alton, 160
Stow, Ken, 160
Stow, Stuart, 179

Tea in China: the History of China's National Drink, John C. Evans, 169
Temple University, 20
Thatcher, Patricia, 43–48

Thompson, Tonia, 176
Tillstrom, Louise, 131–33, 139, 159, 166, 167
Time Machine, The, Alexander Hartdegen, 191
Tomalinas, Shane, 71–72
Tompkins, Ken, 159
Topographical Map of Atlantic County, F. W. Beers (1872), 167
Toth, Joe, 167
Trematerra, Gianna, 4, *19*, *30–32*, *107–108*, *121*, *153–56*
Trip to Mars, A, Charles K. Landis, 135–36

Vail, Ginny, 159, 160, 161
Vassallo, Robert, *25–26*, *109–114*
Verne, Jules, 135

Wadley, Natalie, 43–48
Waggenhoffer, Joe, Father, 174

Wagner, Frank, 161, 165
Warner, Ruth, 162
Weinstein, Ruth, 115–16
Wells, H. G., 135, 191
Wendling, Frank, *27–29*, *53–54*
Wessler, John, 162
West, Charles "Skip," 183
White, George, *41–42*, *131–33*
Wilson, Charles "Budd," Jr., 103–104
Wilson, Charles "Budd," Sr., 103–104
Wilson, H. W., 169
Women's Coalition Newsletter collection, 57, 167
Wordsworth (library newsletter), 70

Z Group, 181
Zangrilli, Nick, *61–64*, *71–72*

"I don't think that libraries are as valued as they should be." (Charla Comer, 80)

"I think of a library as a space, and I'll leave that broad – virtual, physical, whatever it is – it is a space where someone can work with information in a dynamic way to reach a certain academic goal." (Eric Jeitner, 111)

www.ingramcontent.com/pod-product-compliance
Lightning Source LLC
Chambersburg PA
CBHW051548220426
43671CB00021B/2977